THE PERSISTENCE
OF HUMAN PASSIONS:
MANUEL MUJICA LAINEZ'S
SATIRICAL NEO-MODERNISM

GEORGE O. SCHANZER

THE PERSISTENCE OF HUMAN PASSIONS: MANUEL MUJICA LAINEZ'S SATIRICAL NEO-MODERNISM

TAMESIS BOOKS LIMITED
LONDON

Colección Támesis
SERIE A - MONOGRAFIAS, CXIX

© Copyright by Tamesis Books Limited. London, 1986
ISBN 0 7293 0233 4
Library of Congress Catalog Card Number: 86-50075

PQ
7797
.M74
Z87
1986

DISTRIBUTORS:

Spain:
 Editorial Castalia,
 Zurbano, 39,
 28010 Madrid

United States and Canada:
 Longwood Publishing Group, Inc.,
 51 Washington Street,
 Dover, New Hampshire 03820, U.S.A.

Great Britain and rest of the world:
 Grant and Cutler Ltd.,
 55-57 Great Marlborough Street,
 London W1V 2AY

Depósito legal: M. 11568-1986

Printed in Spain by Talleres Gráficos de SELECCIONES GRÁFICAS
Carretera de Irún, km. 11,500 - 28049 Madrid

for
TAMESIS BOOKS LIMITED
LONDON

To My Wife and Children

CONTENTS

	PAGE
PREFACE	11
1. MUJICA LÁINEZ AND HIS TIME	15
2. THE MAKING OF A NOVELIST	24
3. THE SAGA OF BUENOS AIRES	46
4. THE UNIVERSALIST PHASE	79
5. COMING HOME	108
6. LAST WORKS	131
7. CONCLUSION: A SATIRICAL NEO-MODERNISM	143
BIBLIOGRAPHY	147
INDEX	151

PREFACE

Manuel Mujica Láinez (1910-1984), of Argentina, presents the unusual case of a successful Spanish American writer who does not seem to belong to any literary group, so much so that a Spanish commentator called his narrative «... un mundo, un país propio».[1] At the same time there is no doubt that Mujica Láinez is an exponent of that cosmopolitan Argentina which has its eyes set on Europe.

He arrived too late on the literary scene to be part of the avantgarde, criollista, and social trends in the period between the wars. When he began to flourish, after the Second World War, he availed himself of some fantastic and supernatural elements in his fiction, yet did not become a «magic realist». He shunned the experimentation of the Spanish American novelists of the so-called «boom», but succeeded, nonetheless, to the point of sharing the John F. Kennedy Prize of 1964 with Julio Cortázar, one of the foremost innovators. Mujica Láinez has also avoided political commitment at a time when commitment or controversy tend to increase a writer's recognition.

In spite of this lack of affiliation Mujica Láinez has become an increasingly important figure both at home and abroad. He has always been a favorite of the reading public in his country and Hispanists associated him with his «Saga of Buenos Aires», the series of books he wrote in the 1950s. But the success of his works with a foreign setting, in the following period, earned the novelist some international acclaim, which has grown especially in recent years. Mujica Láinez continued to write fiction and his books are being issued and re-issued in Argentina and in Spain in increasingly large printings. The publication of his Obras completas *has reached Volume V, including works through 1957. With Jorge Luis Borges, Mujica Láinez was one of the celebrated survivors of an old establishment.*

His name appears on fifty-odd works. Twenty of them are novels or collections of short stories. The present study is focussed on these fictional writings; others —essays, biography, and poetry— will be considered in relation to the evolution of Mujica Láinez as an author of prose fiction.

---

[1] LUIS ANTONIO DE VILLENA, «Inicio de exploración del país: Mujica Láinez», *Insula*, 340 (1975), 3.

His editions of other writers, translations of plays, seven art books, compilations of travel chronicles, and three volumes of what I would like to call «urban travel books» (pictures with accompanying text) will be mentioned only as part of his overall development.

Bomarzo, *the novel which won the Kennedy Prize, was translated into several languages; so were some of the short stories of Mujica Láinez. The opera based on* Bomarzo *was first performed in the United States and has become the only Latin American opera in the current international repertoire.* El unicornio *appeared in English as* The Wandering Unicorn. *Also, a number of critical studies on the Argentine writer have become available, though almost exclusively in Spanish.*[2] *A basic and comprehensive scrutiny is still lacking in any language and I hope the present study will fill this gap. Inasmuch as many of the author's earlier works were not readily accessible to the Hispanic public until recently and —undeservedly— he is still little known in the English-speaking world, this study will demand a greater emphasis on descriptive analysis than a less productive, more widely known writer would require.*

In the first chapter the life and work of Mujica Láinez will be placed within the framework of the Argentina of his time. This will be followed by an examination of his writings prior to his turning to prose fiction. Chapter 3 is devoted to his works with a local setting, published from 1949 to 1957. Another step in his evolution is seen in the historical trilogy and linked tales, written in the 1960s and early 1970s, with broadest spatial and temporal coordinates. A fifth chapter will analyze the works Mujica Láinez wrote after his return to native scenarios. Chapter 6 will deal with his latest books. Finally, I shall assay the accomplishments of the Argentine writer who seems to defy current categorization in Hispanic letters by his peculiar world view and a penchant for patterns of an earlier period.

I am especially grateful for the friendship and assistance Manuel Mujica Láinez had given me in the last decade of his life. His advice and correction of factual errors have been invaluable. Our prolonged correspondence and pleasant visits in Buenos Aires and in the country have also been very helpful. In this connection I wish to acknowledge the financial and moral assistance of the Organization of American States, which enabled me to travel to Argentina and to devote three very full months of 1976 to research this first comprehensive study of Mujica Láinez. I am also indebted to the officers and the staff of the Argentine Academy of Letters and of La Nación, *who made their library and archives available to me. Other institutional collections and facilities in Buenos Aires, too*

---

[2] Mujica Láinez has been the subject of two American dissertations (ANITA WAGMAN: Michigan State; EDUARDO FONT: UCLA) and one French one (Sorbonne: CECILIA DELACRE CAPESTANY). I am not aware of any Latin American theses.

PREFACE

numerous to mention, also provided valuable assistance. Finally, I wish to thank my colleagues Bruno Arcudi, Wilma Newberry, and Alan Soons, as well as Richard Mitchell, for commenting on portions of the manuscript in the making. A grant from the Julian Park Fund of the State University of New York at Buffalo contributed to the happy conclusion of this project.

GEORGE O. SCHANZER

State University of New York at Buffalo.

1

MUJICA LAINEZ AND HIS TIME

When in 1974 Jorge Luis Borges dedicated a sonnet to an old friend, terminating in the lines «Manuel Mujica Láinez, alguna vez tuvimos / Una patria —¿recuerdas?— y los dos la perdimos»,[1] he nostalgically expressed the malaise of the Argentine intellectual in the face of permanent crisis and the loss of the country's greatness in the course of our century.

I. From the Centennial to 1930

At the time Mujica Láinez was born, on 11 September 1910, an Argentina prosperous and sure of her destiny celebrated the centenary of her independence. Immigration from Europe was at its peak, Buenos Aires was the cultural mecca of South America, and, while the conservative president Roque Sáenz Peña universalized suffrage, an oligarchy of families of Hispanic descent was firmly entrenched and would continue to control the country up to the 1940s.[2] The son of Manuel Mujica Farías, a lawyer, and Lucía Láinez Varela belonged to this élite and counted among his forbears the most cultured and creative names of the River Plate republics.[3] Both his parents had been writers, but it is on his mother's side that we find the Canés, the Varelas, Andrades, and Wrights. Through one ancestor the contemporary Argentine narrator and academician traces his origins to Juan de Garay, the second founder of Buenos Aires. This nearly totally Castilian and Basque family background was a cause of both pride and amusement for Mujica Láinez, who as a scion of a cosmo-

---

[1] Jorge Luis Borges, *La moneda de hierro* (Buenos Aires, 1976), p. 49.
[2] Information on Argentina's socio-political history is based mainly on four penetrating, albeit not very recent, studies: Thomas McGann, *Argentina, the Divided Land* (Princeton, N.J., 1966); James R. Scobie, *Argentina, A City and a Nation* (New York, 1971); Lewis Hanke, *Contemporary Latin America, A Short History* (Princeton, N.J., 1968); and H. Ernest Lewald, *Argentina, Análisis y autoanálisis* (Buenos Aires, 1969); as well as on four visits to the country.
[3] A hand-drawn family-tree was furnished by the writer, signed and dated 31 January 1978.

politan ruling class was equally at home in England, France, Italy and Greece and familiar with their art and literature.

When he was a boy, in 1916, the middle-class Radicals, under Irigoyen, came into power. But this did not affect the country's economic and social system: the wealthy upper class continued to spend money freely in Paris, where the rich Argentine became a legendary and literary figure.[4] Therefore it was only natural for young Manuel and his brother to live with their parents in France, in or near Paris, and to attend private school there in the prosperous 1920s. During those three years his parents exposed him to the most varied cultural experiences, such as a visit to the tomb of Marie Bashkirtsev —a must for the Modernists of yore— and to much classical French theater, an experience which was later to produce the writer's only ventures in the dramatic genre, in translations from Racine and Molière. But «Manucho» (as even in old age Mujica Láinez was still affectionately called by his friends) also lived some time in England, where a relative was on an extended diplomatic assignment. An evocation of that stay in London was incorporated in a volume of essays.[5]

Mujica Láinez was back in Buenos Aires during the second half of the presidency of Marcelo T. Alvear (1922-1928), one of whose relatives, Ana María de Alvear Ortiz Basualdo, he was to marry in the next decade, thus further linking two prominent families. The literary groupings of the period between the wars found young Manuel closer to the Florida circle of writers than to the socially committed authors of the Boedo group,[6] but both he and Borges insisted that they did not even know of the existence of such divisions. Mujica Láinez, of course, was still in his teens, yet he published a number of short poetic and prose items in 1927 and 1928. In the latter year he enrolled in the Law School, probably to please his father; however he did not follow his father's profession and dropped out after two years. He contributed to newspapers, including *La Nación,* initiating a life-long association with one of the Hispanic world's oldest and most prestigious dailies.

While Mujica Láinez started his writing career, the old world around him collapsed. The crash of 1929 led to the military coup of 1930 which «merely ripped off the façade of democracy».[7] The country's inherent divisions, between the metropolis and the hinterland, between the creole aristocracy and the first and second-generation immigrants now in the majority, between traditionalism and cosmopolitanism, among other dicho-

---

[4] See HANKE, p. 169.
[5] *Los porteños* (Buenos Aires, 1979), pp. 50-54.
[6] On these literary circles, among others see SANTIAGO ROJAS, «Enrique Amorim y el Grupo de Florida», *Revista de Estudios Hispánicos,* 16 (1982), 181-89, especially its bibliography.
[7] SCOBIE, p. 207.

tomies, could no longer be swept under the rug. The great essayist Martínez Estrada wrote: «El país... que se nos mostraba bajo un atavío suntuoso, lo vemos ahora agobiado y agotado desnudándose para un examen clínico, en un quirófano poblado de malos cirujanos y buenos estudiantes.»[8]

II. TOWARDS PERÓN

The instability and stagnation of the 1930s caused many Argentine intellectuals to turn introspective or rebellious. Mujica Láinez, like an earlier Modernist generation in an age of spiritual crisis, turned to retrospect. The control of his class was slipping, the class that the American historian Hanke aptly described as «the educated, progressive elite who administered the nation, as their patrimony, from the floor of congress or the stock exchange or over an afternoon brandy at the Jockey Club, the Club del Progreso, or the Círculo de Armas».[9] Mujica Láinez was soon to become the accomplished recorder of this elite —with its incredible opulence of country villas, city mansions, fantastic collections of European art— and also the chronicler of its decadence. In a «Divided Land»,[10] he concerned himself almost exclusively with one of the two Argentinas, the Argentina of the urban elite.

The governments of the 1930s maintained a conservative stance. In one of them, in 1931, the young writer temporarily served in the Ministry of Agriculture and Stock Farming. Family ties may have secured him that assignment for which he was ill prepared. His immediate family had long before lost the estates it had owned. But a year later Mujica Láinez found his vocation when he joined the staff of *La Nación* which he was to serve thirty-seven years until retirement. His duties were journalistic, yet while a «redactor de crónicas» and «cronista viajero» he also contributed literary items. It was quite a variety of assignments, from covering the ocean crossing of the Graf Zeppelin to the reviewing of fine arts. In due course he became the art critic of *La Nación*.

At age twenty-six he published his first book, *Glosas castellanas*, which evoke by literary re-creation a Spain of long ago and are reminiscent of the writings of Azorín. He also received the first award, the Medal of the Spanish Cultural Institute on the four-hundredth anniversary of the first founding of the city of Buenos Aires (1536). In 1937 he wrote a lyrical essay about the city in the seventeenth century which evolved into a novel, *Don Galaz de Buenos Aires,* published in the following year. Admittedly under the influence of the famous *La gloria de don Ramiro,*

---

[8] Discurso de Ezequiel Martínez Estrada en la SADE, en «25 aniversario de la *Radiografía de la Pampa*», *La Gaceta* (México), 5, No. 53 (1959), 1.
[9] HANKE, p. 174.
[10] See the title of the MCGANN work.

of 1908, by Larreta, the first novelistic venture of Mujica Láinez likewise received a prize, from the Numismatic Society. The young author continued exploring the past in articles, sketches, and poems. He felt akin to an earlier generation which he extolled in a significant essay. «Aspectos de la Generación de 1880»[11] is basic to the understanding of Mujica Láinez's retrospect. (It was inexplicably omitted from his 1979 compilation, *Los porteños.*) It called Cané, the Younger —whose chair Mujica was to occupy later in the Academy—, Groussac, Wilde, Estrada, and other men of 1880 «esos españoles de Francia... que se vestían en Inglaterra y se relamían empleando un vocabulario internacional, constituyen el tipo definido de lo que se llama 'el porteño'».

Mujica Láinez also combined journalism with official missions, but the war in Europe curtailed his travels. The fall of France shocked him into writing a few elegiac poems and confirmed him as a Francophile in a country of wavering sympathies. The early 1940s became a period of extraordinary activity for him. In 1943 alone he published three books and was awarded the Premio Municipal. It was rightly felt that his work constituted a paean to the great port city and its great men. One celebrated the Romantic Miguel Cané, the Elder; another the Gaucho-inspired Hilario Ascasubi; a third Estanislao del Campo. But Mujica Láinez also produced a lyrical evocation of his city, his only book of original poetry. Whether in prose or poetry —and he was to confine himself almost exclusively to the former in the next phase— he had found his medium of a polished poetic language.

III. THE AGE OF PERÓN

1943 also was the year that marked the ascendence of Perón, the leader of humble origin who was to dominate the country until 1955. The turbulent present seemed to recall the heroic but turbulent nineteenth-century past of Mujica's ancestors. It inspired him to prepare and to preface three editions of early Argentine writers.

Like many old families Manuel and Anita, with their three children born in the 1940s, moved to the suburbs. (At the time of the writer's death they still maintained a residence there, in Belgrano.) But it is the old Buenos Aires which is evoked in a fine edition of 1946 etchings, *Estampas de Buenos Aires,* by an Austrian artist with text by Mujica Láinez. Perhaps this was another manifestation of the nationalistic effervescence of the first Perón regime, but it is also true that the ousted oligarchy and, indeed, the newer intelligentsia shunned the vulgar present and turned to the old, the quaint, and the beautiful. Radical social changes brought

---

[11] *La Nación,* 20 and 24 December 1939.

Argentina's lower classes into the public arena from which they were never again to be permanently dislodged. Yet Mujica Láinez was ousted from the Museum of Decorative Art, of which he had been an official from 1937 to 1946, because of his involvement with the arts. Like his friend «Georgie», i.e. Borges, who was fired from a post at the Municipal Library, Mujica considers it an honor to have been removed by the regime of the populist dictator and each preserves framed the respective decree of dismissal. It was an age when many professionals left the country, some never to return. Mujica Láinez stayed with *La Nación,* which managed to conserve a precarious independence while other newspapers were closed down. But he enjoyed going on assignments in Europe in 1945 and 1948.

The decade from 1949 to 1959 became a new and distinct phase in his creative development. Others, disturbed by the loss of values and stability in an industrialized society, tried like Mallea and Sábato to probe the essence of the national spirit psychologically and philosophically. Mujica Láinez turned to fictional narrative to recreate the nation's past. In those years he produced in addition to books on art the six works which made him a favorite local author. Later he returned to more universal subjects, only to return more recently, like Borges in his declining years, to the native scene.

The setting of the six books of what has been called a «Saga of Buenos Aires» is largely urban and the protagonists are almost all upper class, but this did not affect adversely the writer's national stature. The country as a whole had come to identify itself with its capital, today containing one third of the population (two-thirds, if one includes the entire coastal megacity). At the same time the children and grandchildren of the immigrants, now in the majority, to some extent identified intellectually with the cultural heritage of the creole aristocracy. No wonder then that one or the other of the volumes of Mujica Láinez has become assigned reading in the schools.

He started with two books of short stories. The first, *Aquí vivieron,* links geographically a series of episodes on a property in the city's outskirts. It was acclaimed immediately and won for its author the Sash of Honor of the SADE, the Society of Argentine Writers. He was elected vice-president of that body the next year, when Borges became its president. In the same year, 1950, the tales of *Misteriosa Buenos Aires* confirmed the prestige of Mujica Láinez as a creator of historical vignettes with an aura of fantasy and sensuality. The two books also inaugurated a lasting connection with Editorial Sudamericana, the publishers usually associated with the Argentine and Latin American literary establishment, even if some of its authors are antiestablishment.

In the heyday of the Peronist regime when the strongman, aided by the welfare-plus-charity machine of his wife Evita, was democratically elected by the masses, Mujica Láinez offered a token and perhaps ridiculous protest. At the request of a friend, he became a candidate of the Democratic —i.e. Conservative— Party in the Boca district of the capital. Of course, as a member of the oligarchy, who had shunned politics, he had no chance of election in that ward of longshoremen, bar-keepers, and soccer players, where he refused to give an address. The years 1951 through 1955 were depressing, but Mujica Láinez found an escape: he turned to Shakespeare. He translated fifty of the sonnets. They were published years later in a volume praised by Borges as the best Spanish translation, but the spirit in which they had been written is apparent in an original poem which was not used to preface the little book, as it could have, after the fall of the dictator. Mujica Láinez's sonnet «To Shakespeare»[12] is an outcry from darkness and fear. It starts with «Cuando más me afligía la amargura / De mi país burlado y humillado / Y el no reconocerlo transformado» and it continues «Me acerqué a ti, que estás en la alta calma / De lo inmortal, ...».

The first of Mujica's «Saga» novels appeared in 1953, *Los ídolos*, and also the first of his high-quality art books, *Pedro Figari*. The novel won the Gerchunoff prize. It was a sad year for the country's intellectual elite. The Perón regime, harassed by unexpected opposition among former clerical, military, and business supporters, unleashed its lowest followers to hit the oligarchy by burning its symbolic citadel, the Jockey Club on Florida Street. Its great cultural holdings, especially its library, perished.

It was not *Los ídolos* but Mujica's next book about a house on Florida Street, *La casa* (1954), which won him lasting acclaim and is considered by many the best of all his works of fiction. That building is never burned but demolished, yet not without relating its own history which is also the story of the splendor and decay of an oligarchic family. Of necessity, «the other Argentina» of the lower classes intrudes in its final chapters, which makes the book well structured and historically accurate. However, lower class support did not save the demagogue and, in 1955, Perón was removed in a military uprising.

IV. THE POST-PERÓN ERA

The new government named Mujica Láinez Director General of Cultural Affairs of the Ministry of Foreign Relations, a post which suited him quite well and which he occupied for some time. Yet his heart belonged to more creative pursuits. The novel *Los viajeros* came out in 1955. Its sedentary characters belong to the same vanishing élite as most of the

---

[12] «A Shakespeare», *La Nación*, 19 April 1964.

protagonists of the following *Invitados en el Paraíso*. Mujica had been elected to the Argentine Academy of Letters in 1956 and he received an award from the SADE. The second of the National Prizes for Literature went to *Los ídolos* in 1958. (The first went to Borges, always one step ahead.) Three more books on painters, *Gambartes, Victorica,* and *Basaldúa,* confirmed the stature of the author of the beautifully illustrated volumes in the world of art. As a result Mujica Láinez also became a member of the Academy of Fine Arts in 1959, under the Frondizi government. He had also begun to travel more extensively and the fruits of these European trips appeared as travel chronicles in *La Nación*. They were not collected until recently (1983-1984), but apart from their intrinsic merits they are clearly linked to Mujica Láinez's books with a foreign setting.

Indeed, no native sagas came from the pen of the author-traveller from 1958 to 1976. Yet during this period he produced six major works of universalist fiction. When he conceded that he would not mind living in Venice, leftist nationalists called him a traitor to Argentina and he was labelled as such in a film.[13] Yet Mujica Láinez was working on a major project, both in Europe and at home, which was not to come to fruition until 1962. Meanwhile, he produced another art book, an introductory booklet on Argentine art commissioned by the Pan American Union and published in Washington.

When *Bomarzo,* the large novel on a Renaissance prince, appeared in 1962, it became an instant and lasting success. Not only did it share the Kennedy Prize with the sensational *Rayuela* of Cortázar; it won for Mujica Láinez the First National Prize in Literature and further foreign awards. 1946 was also the year when translations from French (Molière) and from English (Shakespeare) went to press. In addition Mujica Láinez edited collections of the Argentines Lagos, Soldi, and Villordo.

He set his next historical novel in the France and Holy Land of the Middle Ages. *El unicornio* received the Pen Club Award the year after its publication (1965). Even greater international recognition went to *Bomarzo* when it was made into an opera by Alberto Ginastera, Argentina's best-known modern composer. After its world premiere in Washington, its innovative music and unusual subject startled audiences everywhere, except in Buenos Aires where the work was banned under the regime of General Onganía. But the post-Perón Argentine governments, which came and went with or without military coup, left the National Academies pretty much to themselves. There were no objections when Mujica Láinez represented the Argentine Academy before the Royal Spanish

[13] «La hora de los hornos» was also shown in the United States. According to the novelist, its showing in a Communist suburb of Venice, however, produced a favorable reaction to this preference.

Academy in Madrid on the occasion of the death of Azorín, one of the mentors of his youth. He also recorded, in Buenos Aires, a spoken «autobiography» which even included the words of a tango. It is a declaration of love for his native city, with the refrain «Como nadie».[14]

Nevertheless, the next major prose works turned out to be truly international. One is laid in a synthetic European Kingdom, the other in an equally imaginary Latin American capital. Both *Crónicas reales,* 1967, and *De milagros y de melancolías,* 1968, were structured as linked novellas and he enjoyed immensely writing these humorous books. His parody of South American history, especially, composed in a strife-torn country in perpetual economic distress, points out the value of the weapons of ridicule and laughter.

In spite of his great love for his native city, Mujica Láinez decided to live at a certain distance from it. He bought a villa in the mountains of Córdoba, appropriately named El Paraíso. He retired from *La Nación* and, taking his library and collections with him, he moved to the country in 1969. It was no retirement, though. He made brief trips to Buenos Aires, even abroad, and he accepted lesser prizes. Under a government which aimed at a reduction of repression, the presidency of General Lanusse, Mujica Láinez finally saw his *Bomarzo* performed in 1972 at the Teatro Colón, one of the world's great opera houses. But he published only an anthology of the writings of Adolfo Mitre —the son of the man who had hired him for *La Nación*— while he had three new books of his own in the planning stage.

One, *Cecil* (1972), is narrated by the author's dog and shows Mujica at work at his mountain retreat. With its ambiguous genre, it pleased the critics more than the reading public. The next, *El laberinto,* however, became a lasting success. It concluded the writer's historic trilogy with a novel about an unheroic protagonist living in Spain and the New World in the sixteenth and seventeenth centuries. The same ironic world view is seen in Mujica's *El viaje de los siete demonios* which also appeared in 1974. It is another book of linked novellas that mock humanity's persistent foibles.

The present —which the writer tried to escape by touring and submitting his impressions to *La Nación*— was, indeed, a strange one. Argentina had brought back the aged, discredited Perón. Even many of his former enemies, including some of the intellectuals, hoped he would save the country from chaos and bankruptcy, only to see it ruined further by contending extremists. Mujica Láinez shared the revulsion of other writers and he limited his trips from his mountain home to the capital more and more. He yearned for stability.

---

[14] In *Mujica Láinez por él mismo,* with readings from his works. AMB Discográfica (Buenos Aires, 1967).

After Mujica's mother —the last witness of the past order— had died in 1975, it was Anita who maintained a measure of personal stability. She had patiently borne all her husband's eccentricities, if only his mode of dress: the cape, the monocle, and the enormous ring with which he startled the conventional *porteños* more than Valle-Inclán did the citizen of Madrid of an earlier age. While he was away for prolonged periods, even abroad, Anita maintained El Paraíso. Yet he returned and after 1974 it was even a literary/thematic homecoming. The novel *Sergio* (1976) became the writers' only book with political overtones and contemporary novelistic time. No wonder its protagonist died accidentally in a political shoot-out.

The situation could hardly be worse. After Perón's death his widow was unable to hold the republic together and in the face of constant violence and economic collapse a military triumvirate took over the reins in March 1976. The intellectual community —normally antimilitaristic— welcomed the expectation of a return to law and order, already projected in *Sergio*.

The great expectations, however, did not materialize. Terrorism abated only slowly and, in the process, human rights were completely disregarded. As a result, there was a further wave of emigration of intellectuals from Argentina. Those that chose to remain, including Borges and Mujica Láinez, were accused of accepting an odious regime and lending it respectability.

Mujica Láinez kept producing. *Los cisnes* (1977) and *El gran teatro* (1979) are novels on local themes. The latter became a belated finale to the Saga cycle. In addition, the author began to reap the fruits of earlier labors. He published collections of dispersed short stories (*El brazalete y otros cuentos,* 1978), of essays (*Los porteños,* 1979), of miscellaneous writings (*Páginas de Manuel Mujica Láinez,* 1982), and of travelogues (*Placeres y fatigas de los viajes,* I and II, 1983-1984). The first of his *Obras completas* appeared in 1978. Volumes II, III, IV, and V followed in quick sucession. Mujica spent much time in Spain where he was lionized and *El escarabajo* became a best seller in 1982. He still saw *Un novelista en el Museo del Prado* published in Barcelona shortly before he died, back home, on April 21, 1984. Argentina had become democratic again and Mujica Láinez had a new book in the making, on a libertarian struggle in the country's nineteenth-century past.

This interest in the past —in a bleak present— which has made Borges and Mujica Láinez favorites of the news media, is more than a reflection of Argentine escapism. It is a manifestation of a world-wide nostalgia and search for universal roots. Indeed, an examination of the narrative fiction of Mujica Láinez shows humanity being always and everywhere basically the same.

2

THE MAKING OF A NOVELIST

It was only natural that the son of Manuel Mujica Farías and Lucía Láinez Varela, who published some books, who associated with writers, and whose family history, to a great extent, constituted the cultural history of the country, would toy with literature as a child and adolescent. These beginnings have become part of a treasure of anecdotes that enhance the image of Mujica Láinez as a picturesque and popular figure in Argentine society. This image, which the media exploited and the writer himself liked to cultivate, distracts somewhat from the merits of his works.

A verse play, with the odd name «Las mollejas», supposedly written at the age of six, obviously had no merit. But a poem, in French alexandrine meters, likewise lost —composed in a Parisian preparatory school and prompted by a detention— seems worth mentioning, since it foreshadows the writer's penchant for occasional poetry and his facility in versifying. Indeed, one of his two books of poetry (and one of his most popular works), *Canto a Buenos Aires,* is written entirely in alexandrine verses. Yet, according to Jorge Cruz,[1] the future novelist started to learn his trade by writing a novel, in French, at fourteen, also during his French school days. I have not seen this early work of Mujica Láinez, «Louis XVII», on the imagined life on the lost son of Louis XVI. Nevertheless, the novelist's concern with the past and with mystery manifested itself early in his life; the lost Dauphin reappeared in books published in 1950 and 1982.

I. First Publications

The first product of his literary apprenticeship to appear in print was a poem, «Crepúsculo otoñal». Its four stanzas in alexandrine quatrains in *La Nación* of June 26, 1927, shows the poet, not yet seventeen, apprenticed to Rubén Darío, the great Spanish American Modernist who died eleven

---

[1] Jorge Cruz, *Genio y figura de Manuel Mujica Láinez* (Buenos Aires, 1978), p. 48. Henceforth this basic bio-bibliographical book will be cited in the text by author and page number only.

years before; perhaps also to Mujica's compatriot, Leopoldo Lugones. The poem, with rare rhymes, such as in -ula and -áceo, in Modernist fashion creates a mood and seems somewhat passé in the decade of the Vanguard and the rise of Borges, but it was a smooth start of a durable connection with the city's most prestigious newspaper.

In his late teens Mujica Láinez contributed to a number of family-type reviews, most of which were not available to me during my research in Argentine libraries in 1976, but which have been quoted (Cruz, 64ff). In these journals the young poet practised his descriptive, quite conventional verses, but his biographer notes a progression to verbal portraits. He cites one, on a prelate, which almost seems a portrait of a character from a later novel of Mujica Láinez (Cruz, 66). Of course, verbal effigies and comparisons with the works of famous painters belong to the package of Modernist techniques. So does a satirical vein, which Cruz discerns in some of the writer's first fruits. In his *Genio y figura* book Cruz reprints part of a burlesque poem by Mujica Láinez which fakes medieval Spanish in monorhyme quatrains. He also cites the novelist's first prose publications, of 1928 (Cruz, 67). In the latter, apparently, the narrative combined with the descriptive in an ironic contrast of reality and the ideal. One of these tales juxtaposes the pompous filming of a Renaissance subject with the surrounding present, revealing at the same time the writer's life-long preoccupation with Italy and a period of artistic heights.

From the same year dates Mujica's first short story in *La Nación* (September 16, 1928), «The Mail Coach». When I found this tale —with English title— which has not been incorporated in any collection of his stories, I was struck by the realization that this product of an eighteen-year-old contained many of the themes and motifs which have since characterized the works of Mujica Láinez. Its narrator meets a strange, monocled gentleman in Sussex. He is invited to ride in a mail coach, itself an anachronism. He sees vast estates and a castle, which houses a ghost and in which, it is said, each stone knows a story. The gentleman is the last of his name. He wears a fur coat, in spite of the day's heat, and he is accompanied by a greyhound. Finally, the narrator is charged two pounds sterling for the ride. The old man had nothing left but the mail coach, complete with coat-of-arms. The tale ends thus: «Y él estaba espléndido así, con su abrigo de pieles, su galera gris, sus polainas amarillas, y con ese fino lebrel de Escocia que se acurrucaba a sus pies como los galgos de los lienzos de Van Dyck.» It is all there already: the splendor, the decadence, the ironic surprise, and the pictorial comparison in the evocation of a European setting. It is an ambience Mujica Láinez knew from his stay in Britain, which he recalled in «Los tíos de Inglaterra» in *La Nación* a decade later. «The Mail Coach» is a tale of twilight, not the dusk of the first impressionistic poem but of an age or a social class.

It is quite appropriate, therefore, in the light of the writer's perennial thematic preference, that the chapter devoted to Mujica Láinez in a book by the Marxist critic Blas Matamoro is entitled «El crepúsculo de los señores».[2]

There followed other tales sketching contrasts and the motifs of the collector and of the obese woman — later among the writer's favorites. Also a series of whimsical contributions to family-style reviews, which Cruz labels «mundane philosophy» (p. 68f), and which are ironic commentaries on a variety of contemporary topics, like «flirt» and «grippe». He also quotes other observations from Mujica's early period which show the development of an irreverent streak: Hamlet may have been fat and unshaven; the Mona Lisa's smile may have hidden a broken tooth, and Marco Polo would make a good travelling salesman (p. 70). The same attitude is also seen in a poem in fourteen-syllable tercets, addressing the over-age President Irigoyen. This was in 1929, the year before the military uprising, which overturned the old leader and effectively ended democracy in Argentina. The poem, quoted by Cruz (p. 71), has remained the only political one among many occasional poems of Mujica. Only a few have been reprinted in *Obras completas* and *Páginas de Manuel Mujica Láinez*.

Joining the staff of *La Nación,* in 1932, afforded Mujica Láinez the opportunity to associate closely with prominent literary figures, including Eduardo Mallea and Alberto Gerchunoff who favored the young writer. As a chronicler and reporter he covered, among routine subjects, cultural events and visits of literary personages, such as García Lorca. He learned to take notes and to concentrate, as he admitted in later interviews — and, I would add, to compose without delay and revisions. His travels for the newspaper, no doubt, gave rise to what I would like to call the «I was there» technique of his major works. He also continued writing poems in the 1930s, dedicated to Lorca, to Larreta —whom he greatly admired— and to some of his ancestors. Both in subject and in form, usually the «romance» of the traditional Hispanic ballads, they, too, show a constant in Mujica Láinez's works, the Spanish roots.

His interest in a strictly non-contemporary Spain produced, in the mid-1930s, a series of prose pieces, printed in the Literary Supplement of *La Nación,* which mark a considerable progress in the writer's evolution. The first group comprises what may be termed short stories; the second borders on the essay. Of the former, «Palomba» is the least developed. It is a sketch of a situation. A young girl embroiders a vestment in a medieval castle. However, the fortress has been sacked and the demented maiden merely sees desolation, bodies of victims, and burning tapestries. She runs out to fling herself into the abyss, thus becoming the first of

---

[2] BLAS MATAMORO, *Oligarquía y literatura* (Buenos Aires, 1975), pp. 273-302.

the author's protagonists to fall to her/his death — no doubt to the delight of Freudian critics. In the descriptions there is an emphasis on sheen, as in the Modernist prose of Larreta and earlier writers.

The short «Arcón», also of 1934 and labeled «story», pays a little more attention to plot. It is laid in a rural Spain of indefinite time, in a manor house where a blind old man guards a hoarded treasure in a locked strongbox. There is an atmosphere of fright, both of thieves and of the supernatural. The reader wonders, with the obsessed *hidalgo,* whether the money is still there, while outside life continues normally. In the end, minus servant and key, the old man is found with mere strips of paper, dead.

To the same Spanish phase of Mujica's writings belongs «El Inca Garcilaso de la Vega o el Conquistador Conquistado» (*La Nación,* 17 June 1934). It imagines the mestizo at home in the Córdoba of his Spanish ancestors, evoking them and the Peru of his Indian forebears. Perhaps somewhat disgruntled by discrimination in Spain, he is gradually captivated by the deeds of the conquerors and the spirit of the lands they won. In the end he sits down to write his famous *Comentarios.* The author suggests that the Inca could have been painted by El Greco. (A similar idea is found in one of *Glosas* of the same year.)

«El milagro» is the longest of the tales written in 1934. It represents a great step forward, giving attention to scenes, plot, and characters. Inasmuch as the author considers everything written before 1940 practice items, to the point of calling even his first two books his «academias» or preparatory, «El milagro» was not included in *El brazalete,* his 1978 collection of sundry short stories. But Cruz found it worthy of adding to his sampling of the writer's art (pp. 208-22), calling it Mujica's «first really important narrative work» (p. 79).

The setting of the story is Spain, somewhere, sometime. Two old spinsters live in a house of past splendor —Mujica Láinez calls it «sumptuous poverty»— with an old servant and six cats, likewise of good «lineage». They are very pious ladies and their only visitor is a prelate whom they serve home-made sweets. The old sisters fervently hope that God would show them his approval of their simple and devout conduct. In their unventful lives intrudes a young officer, when troops passing through the town are quartered in private homes. They notice a resemblance between their guest and an image of the Archangel Michael. The soldier encourages them in their naive belief in an apparition and, when he departs, three heavy silver candelabra, a relic of the family's better days, mysteriously disappear with him. They tell the bishop about it; he hesitates a moment but cannot help telling the kind women that it was, indeed, a great miracle.

The tale is written in both long paragraphs and very short sentences.

Descriptions alternate with scenes and the latter are highly pictorial. There is an odor of sanctity, which at the same time is slightly mocked. But the story skirts the ridiculous. Mujica Láinez's indulgent smile in the face of human foibles of all sorts, so obvious in later works, is already present in this charming tale of 1934, which offends neither the reverent nor the irreverent.

Not a case of mistaken identity but rather of hallucinatory identification with a remote known figure is «La divina Sara» of the same year. It is not laid in Spain but, seemingly, in Buenos Aires. In it a young Jewish girl who resembles Sarah Bernhardt is induced to identify herself more and more with the famous French actress. The inevitable clash with her family and her vulgar *criollo* background leads to her doom. Deranged, she walks into the river, recalling perhaps the tragic suicide of the poetess Alfonsina Storni, whom Mujica Láinez had met as an adolescent. (The real Sarah Bernhardt reemerges in *El escarabajo*.)

II. «GLOSAS CASTELLANAS»

In the course of 1934 Mujica also published in *La Nación* a series of evocations of the Spain of the Golden Age. Two years later they appeared in book form under the title *Glosas castellanas*. This slim volume, subsidized by his father and dedicated to the author's bride, had been quite unavailable until it was reprinted in *Obras completas* I. As the first of Mujica's books, it has special significance in his development.

According to the title these prose pieces were meant to be interpretive rather than narrative, but Mujica Láinez endowed them with varying degrees of fantasy and fiction, ranging from eloquent or erudite commentary to inventive extension of existing literary materials. This, of course, makes the book an uneven one, which derives unity mainly from its setting in time and place and the corresponding archaizing language. It is clear, however, that in his *Glosas* the author used a perspective of «writing now about then», as in his historical novels later on.

The first item, «La pureza de Don Quijote», is the weakest. It takes issue with a number of interpretations of Cervantes's novel and also with readings at various stages of reader maturity. Mujica Láinez seeks the essential Don Quijote, the Don Quijote prior to Cervantes, and he sees him as the archetype of purity. This is not modern archetypal criticism but merely a rhetorical musing on the subject. The writer addresses the reader in the archaic, Spanish second person plural, «Ved», as he presents the shining knight as the challenger and conqueror of the seven deadly sins. One cannot help thinking of *El viaje de los siete demonios* in which Mujica Láinez, forty years later, treats these capital sins quite ironically. The first of these *Glosas* ends with a pictorial representation of Don

Quijote Victorious, with hellish symbols at the feet of his horse, as in a Spanish religious painting.

The next three pieces are Cervantine derivations, as is seen in their collective title, «Prosas Quijotiles». They are independent of each other and of varied length and quality. «El cura y el barbero» envisages the two characters of the immortal novel after the burning of the books of chivalry. It imagines them perusing the volumes saved in a scene which gives the impression of being a painting. The two pedestrian personages, whom Mujica labels «burgueses», as the Modernists would have done, become engrossed in their readings and somewhat envious of the absent owner of the ravished library. But contrasting reality beckons in the form of their housekeeper and wife, respectively, and the odor of succulent food. So they return to their placid routines, smiling about their momentary daydreams of heroism.

This short item is not the first example, to be sure, of a Hispanic writer fantasizing beyond the confines of Cervantes's novel. Also, both the practice of re-elaborating known themes of Hispanic literature and the mellow tone of Mujica's *Glosas* recall the writings of the Spaniard Azorín. Mujica Láinez admired Azorín's refined prose, the elegant sobriety and aesthetic balance of which he praised in a speech before the Royal Spanish Academy on the occasion of Azorín's death.[3] This is another indication that the Argentine writer inspired himself mainly in the generation immediately preceding his own.

«Los Duques» is the shortest of the three «prosas». It does not relate any happening; it merely contrasts the elegant frivolity of the grandee's home with the earnest quest of Don Quijote. The knight believes in the possibility of the impossible. It is not his but his hosts' quests which are absurd, according to the writer, and he suggests that the joke is really on the aristocratic couple and its retinue, rather than on the errant wayfarers. It would be an exaggeration to see genuine social criticism in these six paragraphs. However, the uselessness of the palace ambience is seen both in the enumeration of finery —another Modernist feature— and the anaphora of «Reía» of the middle section, when everybody is mocking Don Quijote. An early example of Mujica Láinez's lexical exuberance appears in his description of this laughing spell: «¡Qué gorgoritos, en su gorguera de gorgorán! »[4]

«El pintor de don Quijote» is not identified until the end. It is a real story with some suspense. It starts with an evocation of Toledo in the sixteenth century, in short, rhythmical sentences. The visual image

---

[3] *Boletín de la Real Academia Española*, 97, No. 180 (enero-abril de 1967), 21ff.
[4] MANUEL MUJICA LÁINEZ, *Obras Completas*, I (Buenos Aires, 1978), 42. This collection and its continuations will be cited in the text by volume and page number, e. g. (*OCI*, 42).

is complemented by the sound of bells and the smell of refuse. Then the writer focusses on a house (which an expert reader could recognize) and later on a scrawny man who is reading. Another, thin man approaches, likewise with a book. Number one decides to sketch the strange-looking number two. The two begin to chat and it is obvious that the encounter was never recorded by Cervantes, nor by his would-be Arabic source, but only by Mujica Láinez, who imagines the scene between the knight and the painter and also the portrait that was never completed, because Don Quijote objected. The knight of the Sad Countenance could not be captured in a portrait, but his image was to be reflected in all the works of the painter — El Greco.

This tale was only the first use by Mujica Láinez of the Toledo of El Greco as a fictional setting, as we shall see. Also, the close link between art and literature in his writings manifested itself before he was named a museum official.

«El escepticismo de Sancho» is a separate short story, written after the «Prosas quijotiles». With its confusion of illusion and reality and the irony of its ending, it appears to me the best in the volume. Again, it imagines a supplement to the corpus left by Cervantes. Indeed, it goes beyond the death of Don Quijote, as the tale starts with his wake. Short sentences, even elliptic clauses, sketch a scene which might have been painted. Sancho is disconsolate. After the funeral at Argamasilla the squire receives encouragement by the other Cervantine characters and he decides to return to his rural routine. He denounces fantasy, which he found deceptive and disappointing. «Algo ha aprendido... Sabe que los molinos son molinos» (*OCI*, 50). As the mourners return to the village in the moonlight, they notice suspicious shadows. Sansón Carrasco, the Niece, and the Priest suspect an ambush by bandits; they urge Sancho to seek safety. But he laughs: «Tontería: él lo ve harto claramente... Son carneros» (51). The others cannot convince him and leave; Sancho, who wants to stick to concrete reality, is stripped and beaten by robbers. When he is found, he whispers: «Eran carneros... Mi señor los hubiera desbaratado con su lanza» (51). In spite of this harsh —and quite Cervantine— outcome, one senses Mujica Láinez's sympathy with Sancho's bruises, which are not entirely physical, as in the case of other characters of his creation.

«Refranes castellanos» is an essay. Its language, with frequent nominal clauses, has both a popular and archaic flavor. Sancho is conceived as the undisputed master of the sub-genre of folk wisdom, sayings and proverbs. Don Quijote is a little envious of his companion. «Su fabla se nos antoja un tapiz de colores. Tapiz hecho a retazos, con remiendos de telas arcaicas que fueron de los abuelos» (54). This is followed by general observations on Spanish proverbs. Mujica Láinez, a budding satirist himself, holds them to be «la faz satírica de la realidad» and «Verdad», the word on which he ends this *Glosa* (58).

«Don Amadís de España» is a rhetorical essay. It sees the fictional hero of the chivalric romance *Amadís de Gaula* as a purely Spanish phenomenon, as the embodiment of the spirit of discovery and conquest. He is both a heraldic figure and «superman». Taming the New World meant «vivir la novela extraordinaria» (*OCI*, 61). Like the apostle Santiago, of the heroic legend, Amadís rode into battle in Spain and the Indies. But then came the anti-chivalric campaign of Cervantes, the rogues of the picaresque tales, and the decadence of Spanish power. The conclusion fits this weak piece: «Amadís incendió el siglo supremo con su antorcha y lanzó las sombras esbeltas hacia los astros» (*OCI*, 64).

Of a different caliber is «La crónica del bufón de Carlos Quinto». This longest item in the writer's first book seems to be based on the existing memoirs of a grotesque figure at the imperial court, the buffoon Francesillo de Zúñiga. We are faced with a mixed genre, which evokes an age of tremendous contrasts, first through the remarks of Mujica and then through those of the clown. The latter's status permitted him to be quite outspoken. It is his caustic comment which makes the royal jester a sort of alter ego of the author. As a matter of fact, Mujica Láinez has been so attracted to the clown figure that he returned to it in three later works.

At the outset the writer refers to the buffoons as emblems of Spanish decadence and he lists clowns appearing in the works of famous painters. He continues describing their eccentric behavior. Yet he finds one who was more a brilliant wag than a deformed acrobat: Francesillo, who even wrote a book, perhaps the book Mujica Láinez would like to have written himself. Since no picture of the buffoon exists, he visually imagines him, but he also researches the topic and he comes up with an erudite reference —a rarity in his works— to a real scholarly journal, the *Revista de Archivos, Bibliotecas y Museos*. He also sees Francesillo at home with his wife and later, «Si nos arrimáramos al postigo de las reales cocinas, le veríamos...» (*OCI*, 69). This imaginary looking-in technique became a constant in Mujica's Argentine biographies of the 1940s.

Charles V takes the buffoon into his private service, which enables the clever Francesillo to broaden his satire of the court. «Zumbona risa de duende travieso» (*OCI*, 73), Mujica calls it, and he seems to delight in the clown's mocking everybody with his remarks. But Francesillo's frankness leads to his undoing; he is dropped from royal favor and mortally wounded, apparently at the behest of one of the targets of his censures. The author muses: «fue precisamente la causa de su muerte lo que le salvó de morir» (*OCI*, 78). This chronicle is a major step in Mujica's progress towards a satirical vision of the past. In the uneven *Glosas* it shares second place with «El pintor de Don Quijote». I still consider «El escepticismo de Sancho» as the best of these works. The writer was now ready for more complex literary ventures.

III. «Don Galaz de Buenos Aires»

The year of the *Glosas,* a period of great activity in his life, was also the year of an essay which sparked his first fictional work of major scope, the novel *Don Galaz de Buenos Aires,* published in 1938. The inspiration for the essay must have been a call of the Municipality of Buenos Aires for contributions to a volume in honor of the fourth centenary of the city's founding. Mujica Láinez contributed «Buenos Aires en el siglo XVII».[5] This essay of twenty-three pages provided the setting for the novel; it will be discussed with the latter.

At the same time the writed produced lesser items for *La Nación.* Two, a poem and a short story, are of special interest. «Romance del fin del mar», of July 11, 1937, may be one of the first ecological poems: Man has killed the sea; they restrained it; they stained it with smoke and oil; an admiral will say its requiem when it will die on the beaches. «El grito en la tormenta», of the next year, is a tale of terror in an atmosphere of apparitions and hallucinations. Its first-person narrator is a child in an old house in an old neighborhood of Buenos Aires. Another boy, slightly older, talks about scary things and monstruous visions. The climax is reached in a stormy night, when the child, on the flat roof, sees his friend first engulfed by a moving figure and then crash through a skylight. Marcos is found dead with leaves in his hands. The mood is very similar to that of the linked tales of the writer's Saga of Buenos Aires, as we shall see in the next chapter. The theme of adolescents in aura of mystery —even with a suggestion of a natural explanation— is a reappearing one in Mujica Láinez's works over the decades.

The title of the opening chapter of *Don Galaz de Buenos Aires,* «El page del obispo», suggests that the protagonist of this first novel is a teen-ager whose place in the world is not yet secure. In this topic, even in its seventeenth-century setting, the young novelist had an illustrious model: Larreta's Ramiro, of *La gloria de don Ramiro,* published in 1908, two years before Manuel's birth. Enrique Rodríguez Larreta had been a friend of his parents, and, in spite of the great difference in age, the two later became quite close in a master-disciple relationship.[6] I have

---

[5] *Homenaje a Buenos Aires en el cuarto centenario de su fundación* (Buenos Aires, 1936), pp. 435-58.

[6] For details of this connection and comparison, see GEORGE O. SCHANZER, «De la gloria de don Ramiro al desengaño de don Ginés», *Romance Literary Studies* (Potomac, MD, 1979), 133-40.

already referred to a poem, dedicated to Larreta, precisely on the topic of Doña Guiomar, the fictional mother of the fictional Ramiro, the confused hero of Larreta's book — perhaps the only best-selling novel of the Modernist period. Don Ramiro is a vehicle to portray life in the age of Philip II. He is born in Avila, witnessses great events in Toledo, and, after a dissolute period, dies in Peru. Ramiro's «glory» is to die repentant in Lima, where the beautiful virgin, Saint Rose, prays over his body. This may seem a pastiche of a Romantic novel and, like other Modernist products, it is. Yet at the same time it is an evocation of an era in striking scenes of verbal tapestries in a highly poetic language, with suggestions of nineteenth-century reservations regarding political, religious, and racial concerns of a bygone era.

Now, if Larreta's novel was a magnificent pastiche, Mujica Láinez's forgotten book —it was unavailable before its inclusion in *Obras completas* I— is a fairly well-made pastiche of a pastiche. Apparently the twenty-eight-year-old writer wanted it to be that way. He conceded later that he had had so much to learn from Larreta, that *Don Galaz* was a modest relative of the splendid *Glory of Don Ramiro,* and that he hoped to make his book the Argentine counterpart of Larreta's on the young seeker from Avila.[7] Notwithstanding this literary parentage, which critics could not fail to note on the spot,[8] there is something different about *Don Galaz de Buenos Aires,* not only because it came out thirty years after Larreta's book, but because the first novel of Mujica Láinez has already the very personal markings of many of his works to come.

Don Galaz lives in the age of Philip II's successors; Spain's impetus has faded. The protagonist does not hail from the Avila of St. Theresa or imperial Toledo, but from a rather insignificant American outpost, shabby Buenos Aires. There we meet again the atmosphere of the essay, mentioned above, in which the writer could call the settlement a squat village.

In the essay, in a moment of quadricentennial pride, he could recall the city's lowly beginnings: from the hunger of the founders (to be used later in *Misteriosa Buenos Aires*) to later events, with names and places, with allusions to real documents and authentic sketches by a visiting artist. He also pointed out the contrast between the official chronicles of heroic poses and the reality of patched uniforms. He called Buenos Aires a quijotesque city, whose rustic dwellings gave themselves airs of castles. He envisioned the Bishop taking mate and bickering with the Governor, as well as its lesser inhabitants, Indians, and slaves. The

---

[7] MANUEL MUJICA LÁINEZ, «Enrique Larreta en su casa», *Boletín de la Academia Argentina de Letras,* 31 (1966), 406.

[8] CARMELO BONET, in *Historia de la literatura argentina,* dir. by R. A. Arrieta (Buenos Aires, 1959), IV, 199.

essayist made it clear that he was interested in history, but it is intimate history, the infra-history of his native city and its chimeric pretensions.

This infra-history is reflected in the novel. Young Galaz de Bracamonte is a dreamer. He appears more neurotic than Larreta's insecure Ramiro. His malady (manic-depressive?) actually saves him from prosecution for an act of violence. Unlike Ramiro, he is chaste, even if a glimpse of his cousin's breast haunts him for the rest of his short life. He wants to fight infidels, but it is more an escape, when other avenues are closed, and his quest for El Dorado seems not only anachronistic but abnormal. Whereas the reader may doubt Larreta's sincerity in Ramiro's «glorious» death, the death of Galaz is plainly ironic as is, I believe, the entire book with all its beautiful pastiches, including its archaic language. An examination of some details will bear this out.

The novel opens in the stifling heat of the River Plate estuary, with miserable exteriors and some sumptuous interiors. The page, Galaz, is plainly bored and, with his friends, reads the accounts of love, war, and adventure of *Amadís de Gaula*. The friends are a mestizo, who harbors a racial resentment, and a fair boy of mysterious origin. (We learn later that his historical grandfather may have been an illegitimate offspring of the king.) Indeed, the colonists have an inordinate concern with lineage, real or false. Also the aunt and guardian of Galaz boasts of her background. A widow, she had seen better days in Spain but had found some accommodation in Buenos Aires. «Hambre y hartura de doña Uzenda Bracamonte», reads the second of the serial-story-like chapter headings of the book.

It must be noted that there are historical Bracamontes in Larreta's novel and in Mujica Láinez's own genealogy, as well as grotesque, fictional Bracamontes in one of the latter's works thirty years later. The scene of fat Doña Uzenda Bracamonte walking to church, accompanied by her daughter and servants, with cows and pigs nearby, is or would make an excellent genre painting.

The third chapter introduces the themes of mystery, madness, and death through the fantasies of an old soldier who encourages the dreams of Galaz. This part is followed by one featuring a social gathering of colonial types in a primitive setting, invaded by poultry. There Uzenda's daughter, Violante, is courted by another young man, to the chagrin of the page. Galaz gets a chance to win the girl, when her chaperon, slighted by her mistress, offers the youth access to Violante's chamber, with the assist of witchcraft. One would expect a dramatic climax, but it becomes a comical one. Galaz takes his blond friend, Alanís, to the appointment, ironically finds himself locked in the witch's room, and is forced to see Alanís courting the girl. Feeling guilty of diabolic incantations, he suffers a nervous breakdown. To recover, he undergoes all kind of quackeries.

Meanwhile, the townspeople complain about the limitations of the colony and about inflation!

Galaz regains strength and wants to do great deeds for his neglected city. In his daydreams he identifies with a heroic ancestor but is appointed to the unheroic job of lector to the governor. The latter is seen in exquisitely ridiculous ceremonies which are also highly pictorial. Galaz —like Ramiro in Larretas' novel— still oscillates between sensuality and a crusading spirit. Yet he is persuaded to accompany his master's clown to a Paraguayan courtesan. There, in a scene which brings to mind one in Mujica's well-known novel and opera *Bomarzo,* Galaz feels slighted and, seeing Alanís, stabs him.

Galaz has to escape to the country, where he lives among rude horsemen, the forefathers of the gauchos, until his crime is nearly forgotten. He still considers himself predestined for great deeds. He reads the lives of the saints and he struggles against temptations. On his return to the city, he is stirred by the news of an expedition against rebellious Indians. He sees this as an opportunity to crusade and to find El Dorado. Having become an emaciated visionary he joins in the campaign. There is no decisive battle and the troops return, but Galaz and the old soldier continue. Galaz is felled, not by the hands of the Calchaquí Indians —who also dispatch the protagonist of the author's *Laberinto*— but by his former friend, the mestizo who bears a grudge. This ironic death puts an end to the hero's «illusion of America», which Mujica Láinez mentions repeatedly and which seems to be the theme of the novel, so similar to and so different from *La gloria de don Ramiro.* But the writer had found his topics right at home.

Critical reaction to Don Galaz was quite favorable.[9] Its author was seen as one of the most gifted of his generation. However, Cruz called Mujica Láinez «marginal» to his contemporaries, affiliated with the journal *Sur* (p. 82). The young novelist rather related himself to a splendid, much earlier generation, that of 1880, which he was to discuss soon in a critical essay, mentioned above.[10] In it he noted their irony, their frivolity, amiable Epicureanism, and dandyism. He called them expatriates in their own country.

The depression and the outbreak of World War II brought about a greater seriousness and forced the Argentines to center their attention on the homeland. But the conflict in Europe inspired Mujica Láinez to write a number of poems, in which he evoked his adolescence in France. (They were reprinted in his *Obras completas.*) He also produced a prose item which recalls his *Glosas,* «Adiós del Caballero», in which an anachronistic

---

[9] E.g. JORGE BOGLIANO's review in *Nosotros,* 2nd epoch, 3, No. 32 (1939), 479ff.
[10] Chapter 1, Note 11.

Don Quijote does not fight against windmills but dive bombers, with predictable results *(La Nación,* 12 January 1941). With these exceptions, the writer had his mind firmly set on his city and its past generations, although he would not recreate them yet in prose fiction. His next book was to be a biography, the life of Miguel Cané (Sr.), the father of the Cané who was the leader of the men of 1880.

IV. «MIGUEL CANÉ» AND EDITIONS

Mujica Láinez's biographical works —he wrote three, all in the 1940s— have a definite place in the development of his art. They are neither scholarly nor fictionalized biographies. They fall somewhere in between and there seems to be a progression to greater poetic fantasy from the first to the third. But all are evocations of great figures and moments of the past.

Miguel Cané, prominent among the exiles of the Rosas tyranny, was a great-granduncle of Mujica Láinez and the latter could document his book with unpublished family data. As a matter of fact it is the most documented of the three biographies and, in part, apologetic, as Mujica successfully defends Cané against an accusation of switching sides politically. But it was not only ties of blood that attracted the biographer to the nineteenth-century Romantic. He saw in him a man whose likes he shared. Cané senior and his generation professed the same devotion to Italian culture, which Mujica has shown all his life. And he rightly saw in Cané Sr. another traveller, «¡... nuestro primer verdadero turista...!» (*OC*I, 343).

In the book, Miguel Cané is described in terms of a «portrait of an old man». His home on Balcarce Street, still standing, in a section of the city protected by a 1979 ordinance, harbored a greatly extended family, especially in times of persecution. Cané, too, had to leave for Montevideo, where he spent a good part of his life. Of course, the biographer «imagines» him on board the ship to take him to freedom and he follows him courting more than one young lady. Comparisons are pictorial, reminiscent of sketches, medallions, and miniatures. «¡Qué bien le imaginamos, pálido y tembloroso, alumbrados los ojos negros en una vaguedad de daguerrotipo...!» (*OC*I, 305). Later he visualizes him as a lonely widower, «de vuelta del teatro, quitándose la capa y los guantes blancos, y, sentándose de frac en la sala de la calle Balcarce» (*OC*I, 388). Finally, he sees the spent Romantic in his last days alone on his ranch.

Mujica Láinez did not limit himself to biographies in the search for his own and his country's roots: he also stressed the heritage by editing works of the past. In the same year, 1942, the prestigious Emecé Company brought out *Lira romántica sudamericana,* selected and introduced by him. The selection went far beyond Argentina, including fourteen poets from seven countries, with brief notes by the anthologist. His basic idea is that America, which had lost its authentic voice in the colonial and independence period, regained it with the Romantic poets, with whom Mujica Láinez obviously sympathized. However, this did not impede him from undertaking next a more substantial edition, the «Clásicos Argentinos» volume of Juan Cruz Varela's Neoclassical lyrics, simply entitled *Poesías.* Juan Cruz Varela, distinguished poet and dramatist of the 1820s and 1830s, was the brother of Florencio, the famous journalist assassinated in exile, and brother-in-law of Miguel Cané.

The warlike rhetoric of the expatriate Virgil-admirer and his classicist plays clearly were not to the liking of the anthologist. He called his verses «ampulosos, a menudo sobrecargados por los accesorios hueros que exige la métrica de la estrofa»,[11] and he envisaged a reading of Cruz Varela's drama «Dido» in the midst of the small town which was the Buenos Aires of his days.

In 1943 Mujica Láinez produced a further anthology, *Poetas argentinos en Montevideo.* This small Emecé volume, with a minimal prologue, combining works of eleven patrician exiles, confirms the selector's affectionate concern with a group of founding fathers, some of whom also appear as characters in his prose works.

V. «Canto a Buenos Aires»

In the meantime the writer had started an entirely different and highly original project, the composition of a great ode in honor of the city of his birth. *Canto a Buenos Aires* had appeared piecemeal in *La Nación,* from January 1941 to May 1942. In book form it bears the date 1943, the year of its publication by Kraft, with illustrations by the well-known artist Héctor Basaldúa. It was reprinted repeatedly: in 1966, in a popular edition by the University of Buenos Aires (EUDEBA); in 1975 by Sudamericana, with a sonnet by Jorge Luis Borges as a dedication; finally, it was incorporated into *Obras completas* I. Unfortunately, even a comment by Borges, that he would like to have written the book himself, on the back cover of the 1975 edition, does not make up for the lovely pictures by Basaldúa which came only with the first, elegant edition of the book.

Composing, in the offices of a modern newspaper, a paean to a metropolis in over nineteen hundred verses —couplets of alexandrines to boot,

---

[11] Manuel Mujica Láinez, Introduction to *Juan Cruz Varela, Poesías* (Buenos Aires, 1943), xxxi.

which inevitably recall the fourteen-syllable lines of medieval clerical minstrels— may seem a most unusual undertaking. However, there is nothing anachronistic about Mujica Láinez's book, which became a local favorite, perhaps as a gift item. Above all, it totally lacks solemnity and, in spite of the chronological arrangement of its parts, it is not an historical narrative. It has both epic and lyric elements and the poet's ironic view of history always shines through. Thus, even *Canto a Buenos Aires* may be seen as a step towards the prose of the Saga of Buenos Aires, which was to confirm the writer's place in Argentine literary history.

The poem is organized in six cantos and a brief, traditional «Envío». Each part counts eight to ten pages; the stanzas are of varied length. Every canto is made up of what may be termed historical vignettes. The opening one, on the first founding of the city, alludes to a loss of illusions, which is reinforced in the second stanza:

> El viento de la pampa debió mecer tu cuna
> y el olear del río mi ciudad sin fortuna.
> Mi ciudad, que tenías por adorno y decoro
> un marchito pendón, con un escudo de oro,
> del oro siempre ausente, gran señuelo amarillo. (*OC*I, 403)

The motley crew of discoverers —comprising rogues, the brother of St. Theresa, and a courtly leader related to a great Renaissance poet— instead of their fill found only hunger. The latter binomial, being a variation of a *Don Galaz* chapter heading, was very real, indeed, because the first settlement failed and even led to cannibalism— an episode retold by Mujica Láinez in the opening story of *Misteriosa Buenos Aires*. Then the Pampa took over from the hunters of chimeras, to give way, finally, to the second foundation, by Juan de Garay, whom the poet salutes as an ancestor. He calls the second founding «... cosa organizada accesible, simpática / y hasta casi diríamos un poco burocrática» (*OC*I, 408). The new denizens were largely Creoles from Asunción, «... que se reunían, en verano o en invierno / a ver pasar mujeres y a hablar mal del gobierno» (*OC*I, 409). In contrast, the poet envisages their leader in the pose of a statue, which was erected three centuries later. Obviously, the tone and pattern of the whole paean has been set in the first canto.

The second canto evokes colonial times, with drowsy siestas. Buenos Aires is seen as a sleeping woman. The inhabitants —«alguno vagamente negrero y algún otro / un sí es o no es dado a los contrabandos» (*OC*I, 418)— complain a lot; the city is «muy noble y muy leal, pero no sin protestas» (*OC*I, 419). Unlike viceregal Lima with its gold coins, it has only coppers — and flies. It is visualized in a verbalization of paintings by Figari and Basaldúa. Finally, the writer's ancestors arrive, with great aspirations and empty pockets. Some fight in the English invasions, which are seen in terms of the canvasses of the period, because Mujica Láinez's ode to Buenos Aires is a kind of illustrated history in verses. It manages to straddle the narrow line between the lofty-lyrical and the prosaic-pedestrian, sometimes just by contrasting the two.

The poet concedes, in the third canto, the difficulty of singing to the City of Independence without slipping into Greco-Roman patriotic rhetoric. Therefore, he juxtaposes the formal stiffness of the first aldermen with the beggars and washerwomen, largely black, who do not know the significance of the events. His scenes are inspired in old lithographs and aquarelles, which makes all this very real: a carriage stuck in the mud; rural horsemen —the future gauchos, «Gaucho: gauderío; postre que es manjar de filólogo» (*OCI*, 431)— and merchants, who feel like Greek leaders and French revolutionaries but go to church on Sunday. The dreams of a monarchical solution (Brazilian or Incaic) for the freed lands is seen as a tropical ballet, with the corresponding music, because Mujica Láinez's comparisons are not only pictorial. This is also apparent in the view of the Congress of 1813, with a tono of «*allegro ma non troppo*» (*OCI*, 434). Through the free «Lilliput» city now blows a breeze of Europe. Juan Cruz Varela versifies in the setting of a pseudo-Greek frieze, but storm clouds approach from the wilderness.

They are the hosts of Rosas —the central canto is called «La Tiranía»— and the city is a woman looking fearfully to the Pampa. History becomes a family album or grandmother's anecdotes. The protagonists are the men of Mujica's works of the 1940s; they are cameos or daguerreotypes. A recurring line, «Tardes de San Benito», alludes to the dictator's residence at San Benito de Palermo and the repeated «¿Qué ves, hermana Ana, de lo alto de la torre?» (*OCI*, 448) enhances the expectation of a liberating army. Part IV, closest to a family chronicle, is also the most eloquent canto of the poet's ode to the city.

«Capital» (V) sees the conflict between Buenos Aires and the hinterland, head and body politic, resolved, not without struggles. Yet simple life goes on, in the homes, the dining rooms of nineteenth-century Buenos Aires, which Mujica Láinez apostrophizes and visualizes as a «still life». The city's generals ride into battle —the Indian and Paraguayan campaigns— in the heroic canvasses of Blanes; while her civilian leaders, «Los hombres que hoy son calles, recorrían la calle» (*OCI*, 459), to which the poet wryly adds «sin... el ulular rabioso de las motocicletas». Then come immigration, construction, and growth. «Esos fueron, Ciudad, tus momentos mejores.» Buenos Aires, the woman, «... se va en coche por las calles sonrientes» (*OCI*, 461).

As we approach the present —Canto VI is called «Hoy»— the poet forgets neither the turn-of-the-century dandies nor their opposites, the toughs, whom Borges liked to evoke nostalgically, and who appear thus in Mujica's poem: «Esas gentes auténticas, arriesgadas o irónicas / con ademanes parcos y palabras lacónicas / te dieron (y esto no es vana literatura) / su corazón» (*OCI*, 464).

In «Hoy» the bard of Buenos Aires notes that the successive pensive ladies representing the city really are one. Now she looks down from a skyscraper that is not an ivory tower and she listens to a variety of noises. «—¡Aquí! —gritan los autos que van grabando un disco / en el blanco fonógrafo que centra el obelisco» (*OCI*, 468). This alludes, of course, to the giant traffic circle and the monument, from which all distances are counted in the country. The city, from her lookout, sees everything. This enables the poet to give in to his penchant for enumeration. He notes types, scenes, and neighborhoods, with an earthiness which does not omit the football fans, to conclude that Buenos Aires is a plural city and always on the go.

The brief «Envío» follows the medieval pattern of a dedication to the Virgin, Our Lady of Buenos Aires, the patroness of the sailors who founded the city and prayed for favorable winds (good air). Mujica Láinez's requests her indulgence for the flaws of his work and hopes for his minstrel's reward by the patron saint, St. Martin of Tours, in the form of a piece of his cloak. This half tongue-in-cheek send off is quite in line with the general tone of this light ode, which represents a labor of love of considerable literary merit. It was to be followed by further works in honor of the big city, which earned the poet the affection of many of his fellow citizens, both the ingenuous and the sophisticated.

VI. BIOGRAPHIES - SKETCHES

In 1943 Mujica Láinez published another biography, *Vida de Aniceto el Gallo,* using in its title the pseudonym of the gauchesque poet Hilario Ascasubi. This book not only deals with a popular figure; it is greatly superior to *Miguel Cané* in its evocative features. It had a second Emecé edition in 1955; a third, combined with the writer's biography of Estanislao del Campo, in 1966, and still another by a third publisher in 1974, before being included in *Obras completas* II. In his life of Ascasubi, the biographer uses less private documentation and he avoids polemics. He effectively combines myth, history, and literature with a considerable amount of erudition, since the book is properly footnoted. But it has also lyrical passages, especially when scenes of Ascasubi's career are visualized.

The book starts with the legendary birth of Ascasubi, in an oxcart during a thunderstorm in the country, as a traditional «must». The roadstop is envisaged in line with oil painting and aquarelles of the period. Then we see the child Hilario picked up by the Liberator in a parade and «presenciamos con la imaginación ese galope» (*OCII*, 41). The future gaucho poet was a restless young man and there are conjectures as to his sea travels, with much use of the Spanish conditional tense of past probability, linking the legendary guitarist-versifier with the man of flesh and blood. When Ascasubi introduces the printing press to the old colonial city of Salta, Mujica Láinez enjoys describing antiques there, in the Modernist fashion. He also imagines the eighteen-year-old inclined to love and rebellion. With his guitar, Hilario goes to war, in the turbulent era of violent chieftains, who «peleaban sin saber exactamente por qué» (*OC*II, 69). There is even a meeting with the ill-famed *caudillo* Quiroga, who is seen as in one of his lithographs.

Ascasubi escapes the tyrant Rosas and during his Montevidean exile evolves from «soldado gaucho... a dueño de un género literario de auténtica estirpe rioplatense» (*OC*II, 97). His campfire improvisations in the rustic manner had become political and lyrical verses, inspired, no doubt, by the polemic muse of the earlier Bartolomé Hidalgo, the subject of a brief undated essay by Mujica Láinez (Cruz, 189-201).

Further on Ascasubi is seen as a poet-merchant who «soñaba con transacciones fabulosas...» (*OC*II, 99). With his patrician wife he runs a prosperous bakery and a home which offers hospitality to all expatriates, including the Varelas. Of course, these meals, the hostess, and the guests, are pictorially envisaged by the biographer. The gauchesque poetry of Ascasubi coalesces, in Montevideo, into the *Paulino Lucero,* published first in 1851. (Eventually the book by Ascasubi appeared in the «Clásicos argentinos» series, edited and prologued by Mujica Láinez, two years after the Ascasubi biography.) The gaucho poet's crafty dialogues/monologues firmly established the fame of their creator under the Aniceto el Gallo pseudonym.

After the fall of the tyrant, the now Colonel Ascasubi is imagined in the triumphant parade on Florida Street. He involves himself in a number of ventures, goes bankrupt over the construction of the Colón opera house —which is the scene of Mujica's novel *El gran teatro,* of 1979— and he is pitied in apostrophes, such as «¡Pobre D. Hilario Ascasubi!» (*OC*II, 152), in an intrusion technique, not infrequent in the biographies. There are also quotations of contemporary poems and very imaginative chapter endings.

Ascasubi goes on an official, semi-commercial mission to contract immigrants and mercenaries in Europe. This enables the biographer to depict the gauchesque bard in Parisian settings of the Second Empire in his uniform as a South American colonel. Mujica Láinez assumes a meeting with the Emperor and documents a reunion, in Italy, with Garibaldi, whom the Argentine knew from the siege of Montevideo. Ascasubi is seen as a commissioned agent for various deals, but importing an Argentine willow to be planted on the grave of the French Romantic Musset is presented as a spontaneous gesture from one poet to another.

The aging Ascasubi experiences a number of misfortunes and is seen surveying, in retrospect, the album of his memories. He finds the unfinished manuscript of his *Santos Vega* and manages to complete this definitive work in Paris. Mujica Láinez imagines him seeing the Pampa through his Paris window. The eternal exile returns ailing to Buenos Aires. He reviews his intensive life in a recapitulative enumeration, which prefigures the epilogue technique of Mujica's later linked tales. In a final, highly poetical paragraph, in phrases of six to eight syllables, the biographer has the dying Ascasubi mentally take the guitar of Santos Vega and the steed of San Martín: «Montará en ese caballo, templará las cuerdas de esa guitarra y, sin apurarse, D. Hilario Ascasubi se irá a tranco corto, hacia los murallones donde los gauchos lo esperan, apoyados en las altas tacuaras, alrededor del fuego que no se apagará nunca» (*OC*II, 212).

This book won the Municipal Prize for 1943. In the following year the writer wrote two poems for *La Nación*. One, «Inscripción», is a token of gratitude to the creole grandfather, reminiscent of Borges' remembrance of virile ancestors. Mujica Láinez regrets that «todo lo suyo se ha perdido» (*OC*III, 652), thus poetizing the decadence of his race. The other poem celebrates, in French, the liberation of Paris (cited by Cruz, p. 94). The writer returned to Europe in 1945 to record his «Impresiones de un viaje por la Europa devastada», and he covered, for his newspaper, the conferring of the Nobel Prize for Literature on the first Latin American, Gabriela Mistral, whom he accompanied to and from the ceremony. This report was recently reprinted in the writer's travel chronicles.

Before definitely turning to fiction, Mujica Láinez produced two further works of non-fictional prose. One was a kind of urban travelogue, accompanied by an artist's sketches, the other a third biography. *Estampas de Buenos Aires,* dated 1946, are prose commentaries to the drawings of the Austrian Maria Elizabeth Wrede. Again, an attractive, now rare volume, perhaps a bibliophile's delight, with views of a great city, this time in prose. (The text only was reproduced in *Obras completas* I.) There is an historical progression, because the pictorial and the verbal artists, in their domestic pilgrimage, proceed from the city's oldest quarters to the newest — which is also the route of displacement of the old families. At the same time the book affirms the spatial aspect of literature, which was to be the hallmark of Mujica Láinez's Saga of Buenos Aires. In addition to the use of historical evocation by pictorial animation, we already find the motif of talking objects or dialogues of the inanimate.

In multiple Buenos Aires the old and the new co-exist. There is the colonial town; there is Buenos Aires-Paris and Buenos Aires-New York.

The writer cannot help asking himself: Where is Buenos Aires-Buenos Aires? The old city is compared to an antique, which induces the writer to evoke colonial and nineteenth-century scenes: of processions with «una doble nube de incienso y de mosquitos» (*OCI*, 488) and of oil paintings of «los generales que dicen 'sí' y los que dicen 'no'» (*OCI*, 489). In the next section —there are eleven altogether— Mujica Láinez notes the city's tendency to spill upwards and sideways. The streets, once antechambers, now belong to no one. Trees and statues seem to talk to each other and in their presence one feels like a child again. It is this section and the following, which in some respects foreshadows *La casa*. Florida Street is «lugar para estar y para ver a los que están» (*OCI*, 500). Its peak was reached in 1910; since then mansions have been demolished —like «la casa» of *La casa*— or become businesses. To the South, some old buildings still stand, including the Cané house. Reading period works in the old neighborhood produces «la impresión de desandar el río del tiempo» (*OCI*, 510). No wonder that critics saw a little of Proust in Mujica Láinez.

Next, the writer turns to the North. His memories become more personal as he recalls, for instance, his grandmother's home and her gigantic, oriental bed, which is to re-appear in several works later. He strolls around in Belgrano, with Larreta, and then discovers the villas upstream. He hears the voices of those who lived there. This is to become the basic idea of *Aquí vivieron,* the book that opened the Saga of Buenos Aires a couple of years later.

The rest of *Estampas de Buenos Aires* is a sort of let-down. The commentator roams further and further, first to the river delta at Tigre, where he spent lazy vacations as a child, recalled completely in verse, in the meter of *Canto* with a number of exquisite metaphors; then into the Province of Buenos Aires, the heartland of the gauchos, where he advocates archives and exhibitions in the small towns, with a didactic plea for suburban tourism. Clearly, Mujica Láinez is more at home and waxes more lyrical in the city.

In 1947 he wrote a poem in which the river addresses the city and a short story about an Indian sprite who participates in an historical sixteenth-century battle. Needless to add, both items, which appeared in *La Nación,* reflect the writer's idiosyncrasies. He also began a third biography, supposedly the result of a challenge. The success of his earlier *Vida de Aniceto el Gallo* prompted a colleague to write a poem in the gauchesque manner, which imagined Estanislao del Campo —disciple of Ascasubi and creator of *Fausto*— asking the biographer to pen a book devoted to him. This book became *Vida de Anastasio el Pollo,* referring to del Campo's pseudonym. It was to be the last of Mujica Láinez's non-fictional works, if we leave aside art books, editions of other writers, illustrated urban travelogues, and articles.

Vida de Anastasio el Pollo was published by Emecé in 1948. It was reprinted by Centro Editor de América Latina together with the book on Ascasubi under the title *Vidas de Gallo y el Pollo,* in 1966, and incorporated into *Obras completas* II. The del Campo biography first traces the poet's ancestry. His bourgeois, merchant background meant no loss of hierarchy in the River Plate colony. Again we encounter evocations of eighteenth-century life styles and anecdotes of the nineteenth-century Rosas era. When Estanislao himself appears, he is seen coming from the river, the house of a friend, and working in the store. The Buenos Aires of the time is the «Gran aldea», in terms of the novel by L. V. López by that title, another indication that Mujica Láinez, like the Modernists, found inspiration both in art in literature.

Del Campo's customers were gauchos. «Eran sencillos y fuertes, y al hablar usaban imágenes hermosas. Hacían poesía sin saberlo» (*OC*II, 239). Estanislao is assumed to have read verses of Ascasubi and to have watched him entering the city with the conquerors of the tyrant. In the turbulent years to follow, young del Campo, too, was a soldier like Ascasubi and, in the manner of the master, he also improvised verses around the camp fire. Yet he was not a gaucho. Mujica Láinez repeatedly stresses this fact, ever since his essay on Bartolomé Hidalgo. The gauchesque poets are educated writers; they are city people and like the Colonel Ascasubi, who wrote *Santos Vega* in Paris, they know something of the world beyond the Pampa. One senses a keen awareness in Mujica Láinez of the inauthenticity of what is assumed to be authentically Argentine, and he never made an effort to be «authentic» himself. In the del Campo biography he actually used the word «aprendió» to refer to the acquisition of the gaucho manner by the poet. Of course, the confrontation of the rustic horseman with European opera in del Campo's later *Fausto* —the seeds of which the biographer identified early— is another representation of the two faces, the rural and the urban, of the country.

Vida de Anastasio el Pollo was thoroughly researched in newspapers of the epoch, a procedure which foreshadows the preparatory steps for the works of historical fiction Mujica Láinez was to produce later. This research also facilitated his pictorial inspiration (e.g. the verbal reconstruction of a period «wake» is compared to a lithograph in a Sunday newspaper of the time). However, the writer gave full rein to his imagination when evoking del Campo's courtship and his visits to upstream San Isidro, the setting of *Aquí vivieron,* which was soon to follow.

Mujica Láinez envisages the poet composing his *Fausto* during the night immediately after the performance of the opera. After the success of his book, which identified its creator with the pseudonym, del Campo's life is described as one of elegant society and public affairs. His satirical vein, which is also Mujica's, did not limit itself to *Fausto*. «Le gustaba divertirse, y... a veces era a costa de los demás» (*OC*II, 375).

Eventually, in poor health, Anastasio el Pollo is imagined, in what could be called true Mujica Láinez fashion, summing up his thoughts. After his death, José Hernández, the creator of the culminating gauchesque poem *Martín Fierro,* speaks at the funeral. But Mujica Láinez goes beyond that; he envisages that «Con la flor en los labios, marcha D. Estanislao al encuentro de D. Hilario, en los campos celestes» (*OC*II, 424). This I consider unnecessary kitsch. Also, I do not agree with Cruz, who finds the writer's third biography the best; nor do I believe that all three indicate his encounter with history (Cruz, 96). We have seen that he found it long before. But by 1948 Mujica Láinez had developed a pictorial technique and a formula comprising time, place, irony, and a lilting language to undertake the creation of a fictional world of his own.

3

THE SAGA OF BUENOS AIRES

Both Mujica Láinez and his critics agree that anything the writer had produced prior to 1949 was largely preparatory to the series of works which was to firmly establish his reputation as a creator of prose fiction. Indeed, within eight years —between 1949 and 1957— he published six books which constitute a fictional world, very much based on Argentine reality, flights of fantasy notwithstanding. To the same period belong four art books, beautiful editions of reproductions of works of Argentine painters, with brief introductions by Mujica Láinez.[1] Obviously connected with his activities as art critic of *La Nación,* these volumes enhanced his prestige, but for his countrymen and other Hispanic readers he has been the creator of the Saga of Buenos Aires, the two collections of short stories and four novels from his middle years.

Aquí vivieron (1949), *Misteriosa Buenos Aires* (1950), *Los ídolos* (1953), *La casa* (1954), *Los viajeros* (1955), and *Invitados in El Paraíso* (1957) form a distinct group with shared characteristics. This includes not only spatiality, temporality, and themes but also a technical evolution.

A further distinction, which considers only the four novels a «Saga of Porteño Society» (Cruz, 111), seems excessive, not merely from the viewpoint of an outsider. The six books are geographically centered on Buenos Aires, the capital district and adjacent areas of the province. Characters may move back and forth; they may go from one estate to the other, even to Europe; yet there is always a link to or focus on the city and the delta zone. Mujica Láinez does not write rural tales. If any peasant appears in his pages, he becomes a stylized genre picture.

The time range extends from 1536, in the first tale of *Misteriosa Buenos Aires,* to the 1940s, in *Invitados en El Paraíso.* The plots are becoming more contemporary, as we approach the final social and economic collapse of the old families. Yet both in the novels and in the stories, the rise of the *criollo* aristocracy, in the Republican and even

---

[1] *Pedro Figari* (1953), *Gambartes* (1954), both in collaboration; *Victorica* (1955), and *Héctor Basaldúa* (1956).

the Colonial period, is frequently used as background information. All six books are steeped in the country's history, with historical figures briefly appearing or conveniently mentioned, but the Saga of Buenos Aires is a vast literary canvas, not history.

In this canvas, which can be perceived as a unit —not unlike the gigantic tapestry one of the characters of *Los ídolos* is weaving all her life— the stress is on «Society», not just in the novels. Protagonists are ruling or upper class or seen in relation to it. Any exceptions to the rule are not shown from a lower-class perspective but are portrayed with some condescension. In the novels, the decadence of the patricians leads to the appearance of other strata: In *Los ídolos,* Duma's sharecroppers; in *La casa,* the servants; in *Los viajeros,* the janitors; finally, the guests at Villa Paradise are largely socially marginal characters.

The superior unity of the six works, which will become even more apparent in their detailed discussion, is seen also in an evolving technique.

A decade after his «practice» novel, *Don Galaz,* Mujica Láinez returned to the genre only in a slow process of increased structuralization. The first two mature fictional works are not just collections of short stories. They are books of linked tales: *Aquí vivieron* is more than a series of episodes taking place in chronological order at a spot on the river bank. These vignettes are crisscrossed by allusions, memories, family and business relations of its inhabitants. *Misteriosa Buenos Aires* is held together by a straight chronology and by a certain aura of the unreal.

In both collections and in one of the novels Mujica Láinez uses uncommon narrators and in the whole series there is a noticeable note of truculence and an emphasis on sex, even ambiguous sex. Parts of all the books have appeared in anthologies, but the underlying unity of the two story collections is seen in the fact that a selection of thirteen tales —five from the first and eight from the second book— became an inexpensive school edition, with notes and glossary, under the title *Cuentos de Buenos Aires.*[2]

Los ídolos, always listed as a novel, is actually a set of three novelettes, linked by an increasingly participating narrator. That narrator is an outsider with regard to the high society, which he evokes in his memoirs. So is the narrator of *Los viajeros,* and that of *La casa* is not even human but the building. The outcome is predictable in the latter; it is a surprise in *Los viajeros;* in *Invitados en El Paraíso,* the last of the four, Mujica Laínez, after considerable suspense, produced a happy ending — the only one in his numerous works.

The bond of unity in the novels is family relationship, but the genealogy is left deliberately vague by the writer, who likes to drop names and

---

[2] Prepared by JUAN CARLOS GHIANO (Buenos Aires, 1972).

who mentions numerous cousins. The first three novels are dominated by one related matriarch each, referred to as Aunts Duma, Clara, and Ana. In the fourth, the late Duma's lover vainly proposes to the owner of Villa Paradise. I am not aware of anybody having tried to draw a family tree of the vast «Flaming Tower» clan, but any census of personages in Mujica Láinez's works would be a major undertaking. The overall impression is one of modest Hispanic beginnings, followed by pseudo heights of luxury, squandered fortunes, and an uncertain future, nostalgically but not uncritically conveyed by a writer who harbored no illusions about human passions.

I. «Aquí vivieron»

The title and subtitle *(Historias de una quinta de San Isidro, 1583-1924)* of the first collection of connected tales, already stress people's lives rather than a history of a property.[3] They are intimate lives, although timed with dates in local history. The historical events are of all kinds, the private ones always frustrating or tragic. Failure was to be constant in the plots of Mujica Láinez, albeit increasingly attenuated by irony and human understanding. *Aquí vivieron* is quite grim. This is initially seen in the first of the twenty-three tales, «Lumbi».

A black adolescent finds herself on a river bluff, which was to become the town of San Isidro. She had been raped by the slave trader, but after killing him she swam ashore. She enjoys her freedom and the nakedness of her body. A young Indian finds her, is awed by the stranger, but has sex with her. «Lumbi se dejó hacer sin resistir» (*OC*III, 16). In the Indian settlement, the African encounters the hostility of the Indian women. When the men go to fight against Garay, the second founder of Buenos Aires, Lumbi, isolated, faces a pack of hungry dogs. This quasi-open ending is closed five stories later, in a dream sequence, when we learn that the black girl was torn to pieces by the dogs.

This short tale is followed by the long and much commented on «El lobisón».[4] This story gives a new twist to the folkloric lycanthrope, which links it to totemistic superstition, utilized in Spanish American *criollista* literature at the time. In the story the lecherous, historical governor of the forsaken colony encounters by the river a statuesque mestizo woman and her ugly husband. The Spanish official vows to remove the husband in order to possess her. He convinces the latter that he has lycanthropic

---

[3] The subtitle in the recent *Obras completas,* III, reads «Historia» (singular), which may be an error. The other Sudamericana editions show «Historias».

[4] Eduardo Font, e.g., devotes half of a chapter to it in his *Realidad y fantasía en la narrativa de Manuel Mujica Láinez (1949-1962)* (Madrid, 1976). This work, too, will be cited by author and page number in the text.

spells and, in his absence, achieves his goal. Then, the governor finds himself the victim of the superstition. Locked out, horseless and horrified, he is taken for a werewolf, whereupon he collapses.

«El cofre» pits two teenage cousins from Spain against each other. Fishing in the river, they eye a boat drifting, with a strong-box in it. They expect to find a treasure from the abandoned Jesuit missions. This exacerbates their love-hate relationship and they fight over the safe. In the struggle they both perish and are found close together, next to an open, empty box. It is a story of youth, an ambiguous fixation of the younger boy, and failure.

In «Los toros» a former Spanish bullfighter tries to expiate his passion for the animals. He had lived among bulls, captivated by their odor and the ancient myths surrounding them. Even in his heyday «No se le conoce mujer» (*OC*III, 55). Now a hermit on the river bank, he believes he has conquered the demon of his sensuality with the help of religion. However, when Buenos Aires celebrates the coronation of Felipe V, he is drawn to the bull ring and fatally wounded. His last thoughts mix Latin prayers with images of Isis and the Minotaur. (The latter kept reappearing in Mujica Láinez's works to the 1970s.)

«Los amores de Leonor Montalvo» is the first of three tales connected with her. The title is ironic, since there is an absence of passion. Leonor married an elderly gentleman, who could have been her father, «—¡Ay no, que nunca hubiera podido serlo!» (*OC*III, 70). He kept her like a recluse in a house he built by the river. When her husband has a stroke and can no longer speak, beautiful Leonor rebels. She tells him of all her adulteries — which she never committed. Thus, by the end of the fifth tale, the writer has already offered an assortment of rape, adultery, homosexuality, bestiality, and impotence, an emphasis on sex which was criticized even in favorable reviews.[5]

«El camino desandado» subtly and fantastically links the preceding stories, which, like the rest, can be read independently. It tells of a picnic of law clerks on the Montalvo property, held without the widowed Leonor's knowledge. Some take a swim, while one prefers a siesta. He has a strange vision of the late Montalvo, followed by the scenes from stories numbers four, three, two, and one, even further into the past of the river bluff. When his rationalistic friends return, they laugh in disbelief. There is no explanation offered for the fantastic phenomenon, which envelops the location in an aura of mystery.

In «La máscara sin rostro» Leonor, old, fat, and ailing, visits a relative in the city. The latter is about to give a party for the Viceroy. She snubs her aunt who is stricken and dies. Her body is put into a locked room. This

---

[5] Cf. CARLOS ROSALES, *Sur*, 183 (January 1950), 61-64.

angers Leonor's devoted mulatto maid, who avenges her mistress by locking in a young leper with the hostess, when the party is over. The portrayal of blacks in this and other tales is quite stereotype and patronizing.

«Los reconquistadores» is equally truculent. In the British invasions Buenos Aires is re-won by patriots, gauchos from the interior, and foreigners. One Frenchman seduces a Creole woman at the San Isidro property, not knowing that her husband is aware of their tryst. The two men fight side by side in the battle, but in the victory celebration the gaucho smashes the Frenchman's skull with his rifle butt.

The lovemaking of the adulterous couple had been watched by the children of the new owner of the place. They open a new cycle of stories, starting with «Prisión de sangre». It is related in the first person by one of the siblings, who has an incestuous fixation on his sister. When she marries and has a child, he so strongly reacts to her nursing the baby that he is permanently incarcerated as a madman in the villa's belvedere. The baby and the lookout connect the story to the next and beyond.

The child is Francisco, «El poeta perdido». He is brought up by a domineering aunt, who resents his writing Romantic poetry. Francisco associates with the great figures of his time, whom we know from Mujica's editions and biographies. In the lookout, he composes a great ode in praise of the location, but, in his absence, the jealous aunt burns the manuscript and accidentally perishes in the belvedere, thus prefiguring the «Flaming Tower» emblem of the novels to come.

Francisco's arranged marriage to Teresa is disturbed by «La viajera». One night a passing British lady is stranded at San Isidro and sheltered by the loveless pair. The visitor physically arouses both spouses. They meet on their way to the guest's room, fall into each other's arms to spend their first night of love, only to hate each other afterwards.

«Tormenta en el río» is an episode of the Rosas era. Francisco leaves Teresa for exile in Uruguay. There is tension between the boatman and his passenger who believes the other may have seduced his wife. When a storm breaks out on the river and Francisco clings to a plank of the sinking boat, the boatman chops off his hands in the book's most violent incident. By contrast, «El pintor de San Isidro» is peaceful but weak. It suggests that the sketches of the famous artist Puyrredón were done on the river bank. The story also tells of Teresa's tenants and the loss of a family heirloom.

Teresa reappears in «El testamento», which favors the old lady's administrator and lover rather than her relatives, the Ponce de León. When that lover cheats her with a young woman on the estate and is cheated in turn by the latter with a peon, the will is torn up and the property goes to the cousins. This links this tale to the following Ponce de León cycle.

«El coleccionista» is the son of the new owners, who had eyed an Italian statue on his first visit to the estate. This sculpture is to become a sort of red thread to run through the rest of the book. And Diego Ponce de León is the first of many, more or less normal, art and antique lovers of the Saga. Quite in line with the Modernist aesthetics of the time, he prefers the artificial to the natural. His mistress is jealous of his art objects —which recalls a similar situation in a story by Rubén Darío— and the problem is solved when the lady sits for her portrait and becomes an object herself.

«Rival» also involves an object. An adopted, mute servant girl at Diego's estate likes to make dolls. In her budding sexuality she fashions a life-size doll, which she prefers over her playmate, the coachman's son. The latter, whose advances had been spurned, destroys the contraption and brutally possesses the stunned, passive mute. We have again an in-between age, confused sex, and violence.

In «La mujer de Pablo» the link to the estate is tenuous. Diego takes his cousin, Mercedes, to a senator's ranch, where a social-political party is in progress. The thin plot concerns the host's son's talking about running away with another woman, while Diego observes Paul's wife cycling away with another man. This ironic tale might have fit better in the coming society novels than in the tales of San Isidro.

«El dominó amarillo» involves a masked ball at the Ponce de León villa. The daughter of an Italian antique restorer in town has her heart set on attending the upper-class party and on meeting Diego whom she admires. She prepares a yellow robe and, masked, attends the ball. She meets her man who is fascinated by her Florentine accent. He wants her to identify herself, but she puts forth the condition of a tour of his art treasures. This Cinderella tale has a surprising outcome. Diego cannot comply because he is bankrupt; his collections left before the farewell party to be auctioned off in Buenos Aires. It is one of the best stories, one of frustrated love, European culture, social decay, and a sudden twist in the end.

«El grito» takes place in the near-empty mansion, to which the caretaker's son invites an infatuated higher-class girl for a tryst to test her love. Angélica falls in the dark building and dies of fright. It was not the first nor the last time Mujica Láinez effectively juggled the motifs of this tale.

«El atorrante» is the drunken Frenchman who sleeps on the property. The former engineer recalls his downfall back home. He cannot forget that he lost his wife to another woman, which makes the suggestion of lesbianism the only «contribution» of this weak tale to the collection.

«Regreso», on the other hand, is one to be remembered. It is a mellow story of a pathetic, adulterous couple meeting in old age. Mercedes, whom we met before, returns to the ruined house, which she inherited. She is looking forward to seeing Fernando, retired from the Foreign Service, with whom she had an affair twenty years ago. Her son may be really his. But she hardly recognized the stooped gentleman who «alzó los dedos cadavéricos, con el juego familiar de retrato de Greco que antes era una forma de coquetería que ahora resultaba macabro en la oscuridad» (*OCIII*, 278). Mercedes is completely disillusioned. Her son does not resemble Fernando but merely his mythical image, which she had created over twenty years. She does not even tell him that he is his son and they separate exchanging pleasantries.

«La que recordaba» is a switch to the fantastic which was to permeate Mujica's following book. In this tale of parapsychological phenomena, recalling Amado Nervo's, a girl in France suffers a mysterious disease. She seems to hallucinate and to speak in Spanish about a strange house by a river. She identifies more and more with the Angélica of the «Grito» story and eventually dies, as if in the Ponce de León house she had never seen.

In complete contrast with this fantastic tale XXII is the final chapter, «Muerte de la villa». The title and anthropomorphic detail foreshadow *La casa*, to be written five years later. This finale is composed of three first-person reports in letter form. All concern the impending parcelization of the property. One is entirely business-like; the second is the result of an historical research proposed by Mercedes. The third is a note from a student — a friend of the administrator's son. The historian could trace previous owners only back to 1718, through real estate records. He considers everything else mere legends about the place. The student, however, spent an afternoon there and had a vision similar to those of the law clerk of story VI. He is approached by an ex-bullfighter and a mulatto girl who are upset about losing the statue on which the student leans. When these numens of the site are joined by further strange beings, the young man runs away. Thus Mujica Láinez ended his book, featuring a variety of human passions, on a humorous note, poking fun at business, erudition, and youthful Romanticism. His first collection of tales was well received by the public. A separate encyclopedia article even called it «one of the most original works of contemporary Argentine literature».[6]

---

[6] PEDRO ORGAMBIDE and ROBERTO YAHNI, *Enciclopedia de la literatura argentina* (Buenos Aires, 1970).

II. «MISTERIOSA BUENOS AIRES»

When this second set of tales appeared, in 1950, is contained forty-two stories. A new edition, in 1964, omitted ten in order to fit the size of inexpensive paperbacks published by Editorial Sudamericana. The popularity of the book then led to a third, complete edition, which has been reprinted repeatedly. It is this version which will be discussed here.

Misteriosa Buenos Aires is a conglomerate in an historical display. The writer's introductory remarks, that he aimed to «narrar en cuentos sucesivos la historia de la que nació aldea y es hoy metrópoli pujante, ruidosa, agobiadora, despiadada»[7] is not to be taken too seriously. The book does not tell the history or the story of Buenos Aires, but it is an effort, later admitted,[8] to give the vast, bustling, commercialized, and utterly unmysterious city a mysterious dimension. (Years later Mujica Láinez was to satirize the Latin American propensity to fabricate a mythical past in his *De milagros y de melancolías*.)

The forty-two stories bear dates, from 1536 to 1904, and are arranged chronologically, but they are not connected in any way. Their complete structural independence also accounts for the frequent appearance of the more striking tales in anthologies of short stories. Three stories, «El hambre», «La pulsera de cascabeles», and «El salón dorado», became a cinematographic triptych under the title «De la misteriosa Buenos Aires» (1981).

It is a book of extraordinary complexity. The stories range from three to twenty-five pages; on the average, they are shorter than the chapters of *Aquí vivieron*. As a matter of fact, some are difficult to classify as stories. One is completely in verse; one is written in French; in some cases the relationship to the Argentine capital is tenuous at best; and there is nothing mysterious about the majority. I discern an enormous variety of structures and tone. Also, there is less emphasis on truculence and sex, in comparison with the preceding collection, all changes which made the volume more suitable for younger readers. It clearly offered something to everybody and the more sophisticated could appreciate the writer's ingeniousness, wit, and eroticism. The volume has remained one of Mujica's most popular works.

The large number of stories precludes a most detailed analysis. Ghiano used the device of grouping them historically.[9] I prefer a topical arrangement, since the book is more imaginative than historical. Only nine items

---

[7] Prologue to *Misteriosa Buenos Aires* (Buenos Aires, 1975), p. 8. This prologue was not included in the *Obras completas* III version.
[8] In an interview with MARÍA SÁENZ QUESADA, *Clarín,* 10 January 1980, «Inventé mitos porteños».
[9] In his extensive introduction to *Cuentos de Buenos Aires.* See note 2.

have an historical basis, which is not necessarily Argentine. Nine others can be called «mysterious». There are seven concerned with youth and sex. Five must be termed legends; five involve literature; five others madness. The two remaining ones picture social decay. Within each grouping the order of the book will be followed.

«El hambre», the first historical tale, also opens the volume. It is based on the failure of the first founding of the city and on cannibalism among the Spaniards, besieged by the Indians. To this Mujica Láinez added a plot of fratricide by mistaken identity. There is also a suggestion of social protest in this gruesome story, which was filmed in Argentina and reprinted in the United States.[10] «La fundadora» is nothing but an evocation of the first and only woman to participate in the second founding of the city. She enjoys the deference shown to her by the rude men and the founder's symbolic offer. «La enamorada del pequeño Dragón» recalls the capture of Francis Drake's nephew. A mestizo maiden is sorry for the blond youth, who is to be tried by the Inquisition, and mutely displays her young body to him in a nightly farewell. «El embrujo del Rey» has the form of a letter sent to Madrid by one dwarf to another, offering a formula to free the king from a spell. This is a picaresque item, recalling one of the *Glosas*. «El ilustre amor» concerns an impostor, an insignificant spinster, who publicly bewails the death of a Viceroy whom she never met, whereupon she is respected as his ex-mistress. This tale is one of the best in the book.

«La casa cerrada» is the confession of a young man who had to break into a strange house during the battle against the British. He discovered a human monster, hidden by his family, and killed it on the occasion. «El cazador de fantasmas» takes place at the Brazilian court, where a poor devil believes he can bag spirits. This superfluous story ends when somebody lets the air out of the bags. «Un granadero» tells of an Indian veteran of the campaigns of San Martín. When he hails the Liberator at the news of his death, he is arrested by the henchmen of Rosas. «La escalinata de mármol» relates the memories of a dying Frenchman, an architect in Buenos Aires, who evokes a youth of splendor. He seems to be the lost son of Louis XVI, who will reappear in *El escarabajo*. The poetic ending is unnecessary kitsch.

The first of the fantastic tales, «La sirena», is genuinely poetic. A siren of the great rivers falls in love with the handsome bow ornament on a Spanish brig. When she finally manages to embrace it, both drop into the water. It is an erotic fairy tale with a universal quality. Similarly, there is nothing essentially Argentine about «El espejo desordenado». The mirror is acquired by a middle-aged Portuguese Jew, who has a young

---

[10] In *Cuentos de la metrópoli* (Englewood Cliffs, N.J., 1975).

Creole wife. He is suspected by the authorities and she by him. The mirror reflects the past, the unseen, and the future. It projects the wife's infidelity and the husband's arrest as an enemy alien. He cracks the mirror when he is taken. «El imaginero», too, is suspect to the Inquisition. He sculptures nudes instead of religious statues. Then, afraid of a betrayal, he kills a model, but only he is found dead, imprisoned by the sculpture — a motif also used in a later book.

«El arzobispo de Samos» is another suspect, who claims to be an Eastern cleric. He hopes to bribe his way out of prison with a jeweled ring. When a page steals the ring, the owner casts a diabolic spell on the thief, who dies of gangrene in the wilderness. «La jaula» is the only tale based on a regional superstition, the magic power of the Caburé bird. In it a young man finds his evil brother-in-law harboring the predatory bird. The universal appears again in «La princesa de Hungría». In an underworld of beggars and outlaws a girl adores her brother, who is beheaded although he claims to be a foreign prince. Thereupon she metamorphoses her environment into a splendid old-world city, before she dies herself.

The best known of the tales of mystery and, perhaps, the best in the collection is «La galera». It refers to the covered wagon in which a spinster travels to Buenos Aires to enjoy life, after having induced her sister's death. At a waystation, she sees her victim take her place, while she remains alone in the Pampa. «La hechizada» is another story of sibling fixation to which is added the theme of mutation, of switching bodies, souls and functions. The catalyst is a mulatto maid using black magic. Totally different and quite charming is the children's tale «El hombrecito del azulejo», which would have delighted José Martí. It relates the saving of a critically ill boy by his favorite figure on a French tile. The little man entertains Death until the crisis is past. There is also a happy ending when the cracked tile is recovered intact.

This happy quality is lacking in five of the seven tales involving youth and sex. «Las ropas del maestro» is another case of vengeance on objects due to a juvenile fixation. A school boy resents his teacher's getting married and shreds the young man's hard-earned finery. In «Los pelícanos de plata» a silversmith fashions the city seal. His adulterous wife watches him falling asleep. Then she marks his forehead with the pelican seal and escapes with her lover. «Crepúsculo» finds an aging governor evoking better days. He overhears young guards talking about seeing a courtesan, for which one lacks the funds. So the official tosses him a coin he had kept as a talisman. «Las reverencias» are the problem of a tomboy when introduced to colonial society. However, when startled by a bat, she is protectively embraced by a page. She becomes conscious of her budding breasts and transforms instantly into an accomplished curtsier.

The remaining erotic tales are tragic. «Toinette» is a young woman on a French ship raiding Buenos Aires. She perishes when the ship is set on fire, but not before she is ardently kissed by her adolescent black servant. Blacks are the protagonists in «La pulsera de cascabeles». A blind British slave trader, who singles out the shapeliest maidens for his private lust, is lured to his death in a mass grave of slaves by the brother of a girl who had been identified by the jingle bracelet. Even less fit for young readers is «El sucesor», in which a sex-crazed older man suddenly dies and leaves behind two mistresses and one teenage son. The latter is both afraid and tempted. When they approach him, he mistakes their intentions and hangs himself.

Mixed in with the stories of youth and sex is the miraculous. «Milagro», related straight-faced, involves the sound of an invisible violin in a Franciscan monastery in Buenos Aires upon the death of San Francisco Solano in Lima. This semi-hagiographic tale brings to mind the famous *Tradiciones peruanas* of Ricardo Palma. More light-hearted is «El pastor del río», in which the city's patron saint, St. Martin, intervenes to bring back the River Plate that nearly dried up. The saints in heaven are consulted but not the Viceroy. The best of the legends is «La adoración de los Reyes Magos». A deaf-mute boy who dusts statues in church sees a tapestry coming alive during a service. He projects himself into the scene of the Magi with the Christ-child, leaving his duster as a gift. Darío, who used the Magi setting repeatedly, would have loved this story, which combines the familiar motifs of adolescence, ceremony, and pictorial animation.

«El ángel y el payador» is an imaginary sequel to the literary theme of Santos Vega. The gaucho bard, who had lost a contest with the devil, in Mujica Láinez's variant is redeemed by winning a challenge by an angel. The Wandering Jew legend is the inspiration of «El vagamundo», which takes the biblical figure to the Buenos Aires of Rosas. Denied love forever, he moves on when a woman falls in love with him.

Unlike the fantastic and the legendary tales, those inspired in literary works —a common occurence among the Modernists— are firmly based on reality, i.e. literary reality. «El primer poeta» is Luis de Miranda, who wrote the first ode to Buenos Aires. He has to recite his verses to the river, as nobody wants to listen to him. Even more ironic is «El libro». It is a volume that arrived in port with smuggled goods. It is picked up by a young scribe, who is enthralled when he reads it at night. His jealous girl friend takes it away and uses the pages of *Don Quijote* to curl her hair. This brief sketch, set in 1605, is vastly superior to «Le royal Cacambo», which is a letter in French from one Voltaire character to another, Candide, about his troubles with Spanish officials in Buenos Aires. Its omission from the 1964 edition was no great loss.

«Memorias de Pablo y Virginia» is the autobiography of a Spanish version of the French Romantic novel. Almost a novelette, it relates its adventures in Europe and the New World, passing from owner to owner without ever being read wholly! Again Mujica Láinez satirizes the disregard for literature. «Una aventura del Pollo» is a take-off of del Campo's *Fausto,* using the meter and tone of that gauchesque poem. It has «el Pollo» meet the opera's character in a café and start a fight, only to be bailed out, when arrested, by del Campo.

A striking contrast to these light, satirical items are the five tales of madness. One, «La ciudad encantada», deals with a man's anachronistic obsession to find El Dorado —one of the writer's constants— by organizing a new expedition. His practical brother advises the governor not to support it. A similar clash with reality is seen in «El patio iluminado», in which a young fugitive trying to escape is detained by his deranged mother who believes she is expecting guests to a party. One of the most dramatic and pictorial of the tales is «La víbora», with a monastic setting. A monk assists an old soldier to obtain for his hunchback son the honor of a knighthood. When the complicated documentation arrives from Spain, the old victim of a snake bite, in a fit of madness, throws the parchments into the convent well.

More subtle are «El amigo» and «El tapir». «El amigo» tells of a lonely, starving student who finds a coin. He celebrates only to realize that he had merely talked to himself. The Tapir is the only friend of a British circus clown. He sees a kindred being in the oddly looking mammal. Then, in a spell of self-hatred, he kills the tapir.

The two remaining stories have social implications. In «La mojiganga» a black woman awaits the return of her husband, who went to a carnival with a group of mummers. He had been shunned by his friends when he took an executioner's job. He does return but with a dagger in his chest. Equally graphic is the concluding tale of the book, «El salón dorado», which is also the third of the three episodes in the 1981 art film. The golden room is the last redoubt of a society lady, whose home had been subdivided and who thinks she dominates her niece and housekeeper, whereas she is supported by them. In the end she faces a hostile world alone. This realistic story is the perfect transition to the author's novels of social decay to come.

With a few exceptions, the common denominator of the collection seems to me one of frustration and failure, rather than death, madness, and the unknown, as Villena put it.[11] In spite of its qualitative unevenness, *Misteriosa Buenos Aires* is much better known than the preceding collection, which appears cast from one mold. Nevertheless, Mujica Láinez's second group of stories reveals an extraordinary versatility. It is a showcase of techniques, structures, and moods to be put to good use.

---

[11] LUIS ANTONIO DE VILLENA, *Antología general e introducción a la obra de Manuel Mujica Láinez* (Madrid, 1976), p. 16. This book, likewise, will be cited by author and page number in the text.

III. «LOS ÍDOLOS»

Since Mujica Láinez always includes the exact dates of composition in his books, we know that it took him sixteen months to write the relatively short, first novel of his Saga. In fact, *Los ídolos* was not intended to be a novel. The writer conceded at one time that, after completing the novelette «Lucio Sansilvestre», he found the publisher interested in its development into a full-length work. Mujica Láinez did not «blow up» his narrative nor did he expand it by adding episodes. He wrote two further novelettes, which, combined with the first, constitute a literary triptych. Each part can be read separately —the second is chronologically prior to the first— yet all three are skillfully linked. The final impression is that of a novel and as such it has been viewed and reviewed. The linking is achieved not only through a common narrator but also through a common mood, family relationships, re-appearing objects, and the various idolatries of idlers evading reality. It is a nostalgic evocation of the past, which is poeticized without being idealized.

The intent to recuperate the past —which also represents youth— is already seen in the book's epigraph, taken from Wordsworth. England looms large in the volume, with much of the first part taking place there. There are glimpses of other European locations, which the writer visited in the 1940s on behalf of *La Nación*. In historical time the events occur before and after World War II. The narrator recalls his high school days at the beginning of «Lucio Sansilvestre»; he goes further back at the start of «Duma»; «Fabricia» is his version of an episode in his ripe bachelorhood.

Los ídolos is presented as memoirs of the participating, nameless narrator. But these memoirs pertain only to his relationship to the aristocratic clan of his classmate Gustavo. He professes to be the only son of his widowed, middle-class mother, who stirred him to a scientific career. The latter is contrasted with the humanistic but essentially futile pursuits of the aristocratic idolaters. Supposedly, the right-hand man of a famous medical researcher with a Jewish name, the narrator is fully aware of his friends' idolatries, which he does not share, but his nostalgic obsession with them becomes his own idolatry. This may reflect the fascination of the Argentine upper-middle class with *porteño* high society, perhaps also the attitude of Mujica Láinez himself —an insider by birth— who strove to give his Saga the perspective of an outsider.

The narrator of this somewhat «self-conscious» novel insists that rather than writing one, which could be structured and controlled, he merely evokes decisive periods in his life. He is recording his memories in spurts and realizes that the events he relates were controlled by «destiny». Also, he is conscious of the fact that he is not recreating the past but fantasizing on it with varied temporal detachment. Roggiano rightly remarked that for Mujica Láinez «el tiempo pasado es una fantasía del presente».[12] The nameless narrator of *Los ídolos* and the named one of *Los viajeros* know they cannot recapture youth, innocence, and so forth, but they aim to recover the sensations of the past. In this effort they succeed, endowing the first and the third novel of the Saga with a certain glow mixed with gloom.

The three sections of the book bear the names of people. Whereas Duma and Fabricia, in spite of their allegorical aspects, are real people, Sansilvestre is an idol, the central one in the volume, and a phantom as well. This creates the pervasive vagueness of these memoirs and also the essential irony of the work as a whole.

Lucio Sansilvestre had created a stir in 1908 with a small volume of poetry, also named «Los ídolos», the only thing he ever published. Then he went abroad, never to return. In 1937 the book, a birthday gift from Aunt Duma —the worldly leader of her clan— becomes a fetish for Gustavo and his friend, the adolescent narrator. Gustavo admires Sansilvestre and the narrator admires Gustavo. It is one of those ambiguous links, which abound in Mujica Láinez's book, but there is no suggestion of homosexual acts. For Gustavo nothing matters but «Los ídolos» and its author, to whom he dedicates his entire existence. His friend will have to earn a living, but neither shows an interest in women.

The friends are very close at seventeen; later they are separated by their careers. They meet again in England, where Gustavo, researching Sansilvestre, has found the elusive poet. The scientist, on a lecture tour, enjoys Mujica's favorite points of English culture: the British Museum, Stratford-on-Avon —with a «Merchant of Venice» performance— and at Warwick joins Gustavo, where his poet lives with his English wife. The encounters with the strange couple are interspersed with lyrical evocations of Shakespeare country. Sansilvestre first refuses to be interviewed. Eventually, Gustavo can talk to his idol.

The rest of the plot is conveyed largely through letters set in italics, which the narrator, touring Europe, receives from his friend. These letters manifest such an obsession with «the master» that even the loyal narrator finds Gustavo's attitude rather morbid. It appears Sansilvestre has a secret: he seems to idolize the memory of a friend who had died before the poet published his only book. Gustavo hopes to unravel the mystery of the withdrawal and subsequent literary sterility of his idol.

In Sweden the narrator learns from the consul that two Argentines perished in England when their car plunged into the river Avon. But the book does not end on this melodramatic twist. A posthumous letter

---

[12] ALFREDO ROGGIANO, *Diccionario de la literatura latinoamericana. Argentina.* Part 2 (Washington, D.C., 1961), p. 340.

brings a subtle but striking turn. Gustavo had seen poems Sansilvestre wrote after «Los ídolos». He found them quite mediocre. In despair he almost concluded that «Los ídolos» must have been the work of another, probably the idolized childhood friend of Sansilvestre. He was going to solve the riddle on the next outing.

Of course, the secret was buried with the old poet and «el muchacho de dorada piel» (*OCIV*, 90). The problem of literary authenticity will never be solved. The narrator concedes that he has lost the being he loved most. Gustavo, who adored an apocryphal image, became for him a beloved but somewhat spurious idol. The remaining pages of speculations and psychological analyses are among the best of a writer who has never been praised for depth in probing the souls of his characters. The novelette ends lyrically: «Quisiera que estas memorias no vieran nunca la luz. 'Los ídolos' proseguirán su marcha majestuosa. Las generaciones se acercarán a su ramaje denso de pájaros que a cada uno le concederá su fruto y su flor. Pero mi amigo ya no es más, y mi adolescencia, desgarrada de mí, fluye debajo del agua, lejos del suelo donde vivo, entre las márgenes tranquilas del Avon, enriqueciendo su caudal, porque, como dijo Lucio Sansilvestre, no podemos saber con exactitud cuál es el río, dónde comienza, y nosotros somos el río también» (*OCIV*, 96). The reference is really to the great Spanish poet Jorge Manrique, of the fifteenth century, although it is attributed to Sansilvestre, who to all indications was a fraud. Thus the ending is both poetic and ironic.

The narrator's obsession with his fallen idol induces him, two years later, to resume his memoirs with «Duma», where he explores Gustavo's background. He is seen as a member of a privileged family, in which each person could build a cocoon-like world of his own. The queen of this strange colony, to continue my entomological metaphor, is the legendary Tía Duma, Gustavo's aunt. Therefore, in order to justify his lost friend's monomania, the narrator has to probe the legend of Duma. In the process, as one can already guess, he will destroy the original image and be left with nostalgic sensations of beauty mixed with those of loss.

He met Gustavo's relatives when invited to spend his vacations on one of their estates. The boys were thirteen and the narrator had known about the oligarchic family only from history books, place names, etc. At the time of writing his memoirs he is aware of their vast holdings, their charities, and cultural concerns. The center of that world is Duma, whom the narrator first meets on the river boat, which was to take them to their neo-Gothic castle upstream. From Gustavo he learned the first bit of her legend: a man had killed himself for her sake.

In the country the young guest finds the rest of Duma's entourage: her brother Sebastián, who writes an interminable novel on Joan of Arc; the poor relatives Estefanía and Leonor, who copy, without end, the

Bayeux Tapestry of the Norman Conquest; and Trinidad, who ceaselessly converts genealogy into painted miniatures.

Gradually the narrator learns more about Duma, who had never married, who rejected suitors, and who led an independent life in the great world of Europe. After the boy created a Romantic image in his mind, Gustavo took him to a farm, where her portrait by the suicide was preserved. It was quite disappointing to see it in a chaotic setting. This portrait is one of the objects which haunt the narrator in his evocations of the past.

The relationship between the boys appears quite chaste, but there is a suggestion of an ambiguous attitude of Sebastián towards Duma. None of the characters is married nor has any duties or responsibilities. They have their eccentricities; they seem to act out roles; and they move in a dignified fashion. One critic compared it to a ballet.[13] However, what the narrator remembers is the end of the glories of the clan, for its fortunes have dwindled.

One episode he cannot forget is the time when he heard about Duma's promiscuous past and Gustavo confirmed it. He was deeply hurt and felt the world is a sucession of sad revelations. Then, in retrospect, he declares: «Ya había aprendido que debemos defender los ídolos que creamos, para defendernos a nosotros mismos, para no desesperarnos» (*OCIV*, 164). He realizes also that Duma lived fully, unlike the others, the idolaters, who merely simulated and took refuge «en distintas capillas arbitrarias» (*OCIV*, 169) to escape the outside world.

Whereas the first and third novelette have a sort of plot, its near absence in «Duma» also accounts for the lack of suspense. It is obvious that her world was coming to an end and that she was to die in genteel poverty. As related indirectly by Trinidad, the old lady survived a few more years, in reduced circumstances, in the city, in isolation — not unlike the occupant of «El salón dorado», in *Misteriosa Buenos Aires*. In retrospect, her life seemed to the narrator another tapestry like the one with six hundred men and five hundred animals, which her nieces were still embroidering.

The death of Duma does not conclude the narrator's relationship with the clan. Two years later, life induces him to resume his memoirs. (Mujica Láinez pretends to show the superiority of life over fictional imagination.) The narrator attends a ceremony of the unveiling of a bust of Lucio Sansilvestre. On that gloomy winter day, in a park, he reencounters the survivors of the preceding novelettes. At the same time this tying of loose ends reenforces the basic irony of *Los ídolos* with a satire on Spanish American culture rites, with statues, recitations, and pompous rhetoric.

---

[13] ADELAIDA GIGLI, *Centro* (November 1953).

Thus, the mysterious author (or plagiarist) of a single book of poems has finally been turned from a private idol into a public one. He is honored together with Gustavo —commemorated on a small plaque— by a largely female audience, which is seen emerging both from the fog and the narrator's memories. Only he knows that one of those honored probably was a fraud ond the other, the desperate disciple about to unmask him.

Afterwards Duma's nieces invite the scientist, now thirty-two, to visit them. He meets two young people, never mentioned before, who may represent an afterthought of the writer. Andrés and Fabricia are the children of a relative, who died in Italy leaving an aristocratic but spurious descendance. The tall, slim, and attractive siblings almost suggest a single, disturbing, androgynous individual (who will be reincarnated in several of Mujica Láinez's works).

On his visit the narrator also reencounters the emblems of the past: the portrait, the miniatures, and the tapestry. The remnants of the castle's treasures cram the small city residence, with the blazon of «La torre en llamas» in the living room. Fabricia, too, makes the visitor think of Gustavo. She pretends that she knew and liked his childhood friend. This is not her only attraction. As a descendant of the Dorias she also becomes a symbol of the Italian Renaissance. The snobbish preoccupation of *porteño* society with European nobility has, indeed, rubbed off on the Argentine middle class. Yet the famulus of Dr. Herzberg is not going to marry Fabricia. There is not only a rival, but the narrator's eroticism is largely allegorical. The real world is that of an ex-Fascist marquis in the oil business who can save the family from ruin.

The climax of the book is a scene —the narrator calls it so— in an attic to which he and Fabricia ascend in search of a souvenir of Gustavo. This episode, which recalls one in Larreta's famous novel, is a dusty moon- and candle-lit ascent into the past. Chaotic enumeration and an allusion to surrealist painting seem quite natural in the setting. Also, it does not come unexpectedly when the two find the «Los ídolos» volume of 1937 and the photos of Sansilvestre, of Duma, and of Gustavo; no wonder the doctor kisses Fabricia there. What is surprising, however, is his quick withdrawal. Still, the narrator explains: «supe que Fabricia me importaba menos que la recuperación de las sensaciones de la plenitud feliz... de mi intimidad con Gustavo» (*OCIV*, 255).

In the end he goes to open «Los ídolos». He passes in review —in one of the writer's typical summations— the scenes the reader already knows. The narrator, who recognized the pitfalls of sterile idolatry all along, has become a confirmed idolater of the past. Mujica Láinez has overcome the dilemma by converting the idolatrized past into literature. The ending is melancholy but mellow, as one can expect in a book on the theme of elegant escapism.

Critical reactions to *Los ídolos* were quite favorable and stressed the book's aestheticism and treatment of decadence.[14] Some noted the absence of a clear-cut protagonist and saw in Duma its culminating figure (Villena, 20; Ghiano, 15). Borges, a master of mirrors and labyrinths, found *Los ídolos* structured «por medio de espejos enfrentados, puesto que los personajes están creados como reflejos recíprocos...» and, he said, the work has «algo de laberinto».[15] Others, especially Font (27-29), discussed the echoes of Proust, whom Mujica always considered part of his world. There was no doubt, however, that finally, at forty-three, Mujica Láinez had established himself as a novelist.

IV. «LA CASA»

It took the writer only seven months to compose the next work, which must have been on his mind for a long time. In an interview he said: «Hace mucho que he querido escribir un libro en el que el mundo de las cosas, de los objetos, un mundo que siento vivir en torno, alcanzaría una jerarquía tan importante como la del nuestro, la del mundo de la gente. Además pensé vincular este libro con la historia de una familia, de la decadencia de una familia... para crear una sola y amplia alegoría.»[16] This is what Mujica Láinez did in *La casa*. In spite of many differences, it was immediately felt that his entire previous work had been a preparation for this novel,[17] which became the keystone of the Saga of Buenos Aires. Its central position is even geographical. The setting of *Aquí vivieron* became a suburban stop; *Misteriosa Buenos Aires* only ends in a deteriorated building downtown; *Los ídolos* evokes happiness at a castle upstream; the actions of the third and fourth novels occur at a train ride's distance from Buenos Aires. Only *La casa*, the mansion on Florida Street, stands in the very center of Argentine social, cultural, and political life.

Again there is an English epigraph, taken from T. S. Eliot's *Four Quartets*, which refers to the life and death of houses. *La casa* is the life story of a dying mansion. It is told in the first person by the sixty-eight year old building in ten successive nights of recollections, corresponding both to the breaks in the demolition process and to the chapters of

---

[14] VICENTE BARBIERI, *Sur*, 226 (Jan.-Feb. 1954); GLADYS KRIEBLE, «Literary Letter from Buenos Aires», *New York Times Book Review*, 24 January 1954, and others.
[15] BORGES, cited in «Banquete ofrecido a Mujica Láinez», *La Nación*, 10 October 1953.
[16] In an interview signed by EUGENIO ARAOZ, *Esto es*, 2 November 1954.
[17] EDUARDO GONZÁLEZ LANUZA, *Sur*, 231 (1954), 99.

the book. A final, one-page division represents the last, inarticulate thoughts of the house-narrator, whose viewpoint is the only one shown.

The theme of decadence is unfolded in the lives of the inhabitants. These lives form a sort of condensed social history of Argentina. The many characters, as in real life, go (by death) and come (by more or less unexpected arrival). Some reemerge from another work of the writer. The key figures are better developed than Mujica's earlier creations; yet they are always seen from the outside. The outside observer here is the house, who is quite a «character» herself.

The house is the central protagonist. She —the choice of gender is not necessarily linked to the Spanish gender of the title— has a stake in the events; she has feelings of pride and guilt; she considers herself so much part of the family that she looks down on the later, plebeian occupants. The writer made his narrator rather chatty, eager to confess and to comment. This may reflect his concept of women, as we shall see also in the charming fairy-narrator of *El unicornio*. The comments of the house are seconded by the reactions, individual or collective, of the objects, the anthropomorphic denizens of the mansion.

Inasmuch as the old building declares in the second line «Pronto voy a morir» (*OC*IV, 255), there is little suspense. She and we know that she will be replaced by a commercial construction. This is part of Mujica's world view which sees tomes attacked by book worms, corpses as targets of larvae, and the mansions of the 1880s giving way to inexorable progress, yet all perceived with the nostalgia of the aesthete.

Historically the novel spans the period from the 1880s to the Peronist regime. But *La casa* is not traditional biography. The narrator, an old lady, does not report systematically nor chronologically. Basically she proceeds from «the good old days» to those of total decay; yet she omits scenes and episodes and later remembers them in an associative stream of reminiscences. Also, she is only partially «privileged» in her knowledge.

One aspect beyond her comprehension is the supernatural, which she accepts. Mujica Láinez likes to mix fantasy and reality, at times with tongue-in-cheek. There is no suggestion of primitive beliefs here as in the contemporary magic realism of Latin America. But the mansion harbors two spirits and one mysterious «presence», which the narrator feels but does not attempt to explain. It might be an angel, a guardian of the place. We are left with the impression, however, that the supernatural, too, falls victim to the pickax.

The ghosts are «el Caballero» and Tristán. The former is an anachronistic figure, perhaps the soul of an ancestor from the family's modest, creole beginnings; the latter is the Senator's young son, whose murder is evoked in the first chapter as the secret «original sin» of the family. The two are the reappearing *manes* of the story. The house and the objects are the witnesses of all the evil deeds committed there and they are embarrassed by the baring demolition process. The house starts every night's recollections with a stream of complaints and the objects vent their plight as they face removal or destruction.

The objects also comment on the events, usually tragic, like a chorus. Yet they do it each in its own way, according to sex, age, nationality, period of creation, and even what they stand for. This affords the cosmopolitan writer much ingenious and even ironic comment. The objects also address each other and show rivalries — e.g. Italian frescos and French paintings. One statue even intervenes in the plot when its outstretched hand causes an intruder's fatal stumble. This is not only part of a literary technique but an expression of the novelist's concept of the inanimate world as animated, which further links him to the Modernists and their Pythagorean tendencies.

The house on Florida Street was built by a senator and friend of the president in the 1880s. He appears only in retrospect, as remembered by his widow or the narrator. By a process of modified recuperation of the past —already hinted in *Los ídolos*— the old statesman becomes more and more cultured in their minds. Clara, the widow, is a caricature of an obese woman. She is seen in various stages of gluttony, which causes both her deformity and her isolation. She has a mania for collections. Her room is crammed with oriental bibelots —a Modernist fad— and later with religious trinkets. Their chaotic enumeration seems a normal description of a chaotic interior.

Paco is another idolatrous collector. He spends a fortune on his hobby of paper-weights from all over the world. It was Paco who pushed his brother Tristán from a rear balcony to his death during a carnival celebration. Nobody ever found out, but Paco became more and more withdrawn. Clara had him declared insane and, after a couple of violent incidents, even placed in an institution. The senator's heir is Gustavo, the only normal one of the males in the family. He, too, is a collector, but he does not hoard. He collects elegant clothes, carriages, gestures, and, undoubtedly, women. When he is seen by his adolescent son, Francis, embracing a French demi-mondaine, he causes a trauma that contributes to the boy's premature death. His mother goes to live in Europe.

Gustavo's dealings with administrators link the family to the real Argentina, which provides the wealth to be squandered at home and abroad. But the «clubman» Gustavo and his wife do everything in style and are evoked nostalgically by the narrator.

The delicate Francis takes refuge in the occult. He amasses strange books and friends who may be homosexuals. He holds a spiritistic séance in a striking scene, in which the presence of the family ghosts is felt:

one of the spiritualists faints, Paco, in his room, screams, while the statues and the figures in paintings and on the Beauvais tapestry shout in their respective tongues.

The aristocratic family circle is pierced later by two low-class sisters, Rosa and Zulema. The new servants open up a whole new upstairs-downstairs perspective. They win the protection of Clara, who talks to them about her late husband, converted into «un arquetipo del senador ideal» (*OCIV*, 338). They try in vain to seduce Francis, for the scrawny, scheming Zulema manipulates the older sister's voluptuousness. Rosa first takes up with the French chef in a comedy intrigue, which stirs up the latent eroticism of the old house and the not-so-latent one of the works of art. There is much sex in *La casa* and, unlike in other books of the writer, it is quite normal. Yet it is never joyful heterosexual love; nor is it treated explicitly. Strange words, indeed, are used to refer to erotic activities. The house muses over «ritos tradicionales eróticos» or «procedimientos» (*OCIV*, 314). Later they are called «ejercicios amorosos» (*OCIV*, 447), as if the participants engaged in strenuous athletics. Whether prudish or ironical, these expressions reflect Mujica Láinez's constant of the disillusions of love.

After the death of Francis and Clara, the servant sisters gain in importance because of Rosa's involvement with Benjamín. The remaining son, whom the house despises, lacks style. He embarrasses the clan by being contented with the possession of Rosa, a sensual, ripe, Creole beauty. She is a mere sex object and as such becomes the catalyst of events. Zulema is the prime mover. She wants to control the mansion and its wealth albeit without any knowledge of its significance and worth. Eventually she reaches her goal, only to die a recluse in an empty, leaky, rat-infested shell.

Meanwhile, the house recalls splendid receptions of distinguished visitors, with ritualistic, processional movements, and even some conversations (which Mujica Láinez had not stressed before). All this is related somewhat sardonically.

Half-way through the book the story of a family becomes one of the inheritors. They are no less wasteful and live on the slow dissolution of the treasures still stored at the mansion. Benjamín openly lives with Rosa. She and Zulema soon introduce their own ilk into the stately dwelling. The passing of the world is seen by the house —in the language typical of the author— at Gustavo's wake:

> Vinieron hasta dos ancianos casi centenarios, increíbles: el de la barba en punta que había distraído mis sobremesas con sus cuentos obscenos y aquél cuya protección hizo llover diamantes sobre el escote de Aimée de Monvel. Habían sido amigos del senador en la suntuosa prehistoria juarista, y residían más allá del bien y de mal, en una suave y sonriente inconsciencia. Se pre-

sentaron por la tarde, manejados por hábiles bisnietos que los pilotearon hacia la seguridad de un canapé, y allí resistieron media hora como dos reliquias ilustres ofrecidos a la espantada veneración del público. (*OCIV*, 439)

In the second half of the book further low-class characters appear, who are scorned by the house and by the objects, now depleted by sales, auctions, and plain theft. Zulema first brings her cousin Nicanor, then Leonardo Vagnoli, a *compadrito,* taken directly from the city's folklore or indirectly from Borges. Leonardo first takes up with Zulema, then with Rosa, who is tired of Benjamín after twelve years. In his absence the sisters and their friends make merry, but not with gourmet food and classical music. Their parties, with pizza (with much garlic), and with accompaniment of tangos and milongas, are parodies of the feast of yore. When Benjamín catches his rival, a fight ensues, and Leonardo does the expected: he marks Benjamín's face with his knife. The latter does not survive long the insult and dies without being able to change his will. In 1934, Rose is the new owner.

During the remaining eighteen years the house is controlled by Zulema who acquiesces to its deterioration but will not sell. Leandro and Nicanor dispose of things cheaply. They are busy with party matters, apparently Peronista. In the face of complete neglect the narrating house cannot help evoking past glories, such as a banquet for Prince Brandini, Duma's lover. The anachronism is deliberate; *La casa* does not pretend to be a chronicle.

Nicanor brings another occupant, the young whore Dolly, whom the narrator describes with sympathy. She is romantic and she is innocent of the men's plot to steal a fabulous necklace, which Zulema refuses to release. Nicanor and Leandro plan to make the girls drunk and stage a grotesque feast in the great hall, with ravioli on Limoges china, in an atmosphere of «sahumerio, ... grasa y ... gato incontinente» (*OCIV*, 520). Leandro alone disappears with the heirloom. Zulema wants restitution and sets a trap for Leandro. When he returns, he falls to his death at the foot of the great staircase. The unexplained accident parallels the one at the start of the book. Rosa does not forgive her sister and Zulema remains alone in the empty ruins with its tapestry, frescos and ghosts.

In her own and the mansion's terminal loneliness, the remaining objects reenact the scenes which they represent in the last breath of a dying culture. After Zulema's death, Nicanor disposes the final demolition. The narrator's ultimate, inarticulate thoughts are spaced by dots.

Immediate critical reaction to the novel was sharply divided because of a highly politicized atmosphere. Populist or leftist commentators resented both the topic and the slant of the book, which was felt to be anti-people. David Viñas called Mujica Láinez's characters «cadáveres», but suggested that, if Borges had written a novel, he would have written

La casa.[18] The academician González Lanuza, on the other hand, expressed the opinion that the novel could not have been written by anybody else. He praised its style, its irony, and increasing satire.[19] Twenty-two years and many books later, he told me that he still considered *La casa* the writer's best book.[20] Villena judged it the most harmoniously constructed (p. 21). Font analyzed it in detail in one of his six chapters (IV). Critics noted its lyrical qualities, but none seem to have stressed its dramatic aspects. *La casa* is written in scenes, a term which I have used repeatedly. Mujica Láinez did not write original plays, but he conceded «Siempre he soñado con poder escribir para el teatro».[21] Obviously, he conceived much of his fiction as scenarios.

V. «LOS VIAJEROS»

Even before *La casa* was published, Mujica Láinez completed in less than four months of 1954 *Los viajeros,* the third novel of his Saga. This Saga is not a chronological series but rather an overview from different angles. The picture is the same: the decadence of a refined society. This seemed background in *Los ídolos;* the total collapse is seen in *La casa,* where destruction by the wreckers merely completes the work of the low-class successors to Clara's branch of the clan. In *Los viajeros,* another withered branch of the «Flaming Tower» family is confronted with the new midde class in a town of the Province of Buenos Aires.

Aunt Duma of the first novel, Aunt Clara of the second, and Aunt Ema of the third, are cousins, but what holds the Saga together is less cognation than parallel escapist illusions, combined with waning fortunes. The Gothic castle of Duma was lost; Clara's city mansion is demolished; «Los Miradores», the setting of *Los viajeros,* is not only sold to become the country club of the adjacent, new petroleum refinery, it does go up in flames. This ironically authenticates the made-up coat of arms of a clan which is on the verge of extinction. The grandchildren of sturdy Creole ranchers and children of cosmopolitan upstarts are all unmarried and leave no descendants.

The irony of the title of the book is even more basic: «The travellers» never travel. They only dream of a grand tour of Europe, for which they prepare ceaselessly, but their illusions are progressively destroyed until

---

[18] «Otros novelistas argentinos por orden cronológico», *Contorno,* 3 (September 1954), 8. It should be noted that the leftist VIÑAS, in his *Literatura argentina y realidad política,* 3 volumes (Buenos Aires, 1971-75) only alludes to Mujica Láinez in passing.
[19] In the review cited in note 17 above.
[20] June 21, 1976, in the Argentine Academy of Letters.
[21] ARAOZ interview, note 16 above.

they themselves are destroyed. They perish just when Aunt Ema, who has supported the poor relatives all along, announces the financing of their trip from the sale of the estate. However, these plot elements do not make up the theme of the book. They underline the social decay, ever present in the saga; yet in the third novel the writer skilfully clothed it in a bitter-sweet love story. This makes *Los viajeros* almost unique, in spite of its links to and similarities with his other works. One could call it a «rite of passage» book, which includes the theme of lost innocence, but the normal, pure relationship between Miguel and Berenice has no counterpart in Mujica Láinez's fiction. It can only end tragically and it does.

It is all told by Miguel in his notebooks, which make up the novel, in eleven sections. He is a dramatized narrator, who evokes past events some time after their melodramatic finale. He, too, is an outsider, both at «Los Miradores», as an orphan and bastard relative, and, for Berenice's bourgeois family, as a member of the aristocratic clan. This enables him to view both worlds with some detachment. Also, his interest in poetry makes this narrator similar to that of *Los ídolos* and a spokesman for the writer.

Whereas the immovable «travellers» are all adults, the book is really a novel of adolescence. It is the nostalgic evocation of Miguel's youth at «Los Miradores». His only «trip» is the «paradójico viaje retrospectivo de viajero condenado a no moverse».[22] Growing up is not easy for the narrator protagonist, who is the only young person in a household of odd spinsters and bachelors. Their only common aim is to return to the Old World, which they had seen in better days.[23]

Locally, they try to uphold the prestige of the founding family of the settlement, although they depend entirely on distant Aunt Ema, and Miguel in turn depends on them. His mother had been a rebellious member of the clan, who ran away with a Polish juggler — a real traveller. Soon after the boy's birth his parents were killed in an automobile accident abroad and Miguel was raised by his mother's unmarried siblings. There is something unconventional about this participating narrator, who is a kept nephew of kept relatives, whose name is foreign, whose father was a magician, and who writes poetry. He has something of the artist-protagonist of Modernist fiction. Indeed, he is sensitive to all aspects of beauty.

The setting is a villa by the river in an unnamed town of the Province

---

[22] MANUEL MUJICA LÁINEZ, *Los viajeros* (Buenos Aires, 1967), p. 8. Further reference to this novel will be taken from the fifth volume of *Obras completas*, now available.
[23] Cf. «El viaje a Europa» chapter in VIÑA's Volume I (note 18 above), on this social pattern, albeit without allusion to Mujica's novel.

of Buenos Aires. Much of the founding grandfather's estate had already been sold to the refinery, which looms menacingly over «Los Miradores». This plant clearly symbolizes the encroachment of the industrial world and its eventual explosion destroys the villa, devastates part of the town, and produces the tragic dénouement of the novel. School, church, and central square of the community are alternate locations, as Miguel's love for Berenice links «Los Mirasoles» with the other word of the middle class.

The villa itself has something of *La casa,* since it is used only in part. Its richly furnished main section is vacant and locked, under the care of servants, while Aunt Ema's poor relatives occupy lesser quarters. Thus there is a forbidden zone, as in the «Grito» story of *Aquí vivieron.* There are also a dilapidated greenhouse and a carriage house, which are the scenes of significant episodes. In these musty settings Miguel's only childhood companion is Simón, the son of the guardians of the place. The novelistic time of their teens appears to be the historical one between the wars.

The novel's epigraph is taken from Racine's *Berenice* and foreshadows not only the name of the heroine —called one of the most delightful characters of Argentine fiction by one of the critics[24]— but also an abortive ending. The French quotation reflects the novelist's love for the classical theater, which led to his translating Racine's *Fedra* in the next decade. The second Old World influence is Italian, since Berenice is the daughter of an Italian pianist and Miguel first spots her in a Renaissance costume, which she donned for a «Romeo and Juliet» ballet scene, staged by Aunt Elisa. Of course, European culture permeates the entire book with the travel motif. Fermín, Elisa, Baltasar, and Gertrudis constantly discuss alternate itineraries and Miguel is made to spend endless hours on guide books and art histories. While he resents the obligatory aspect of these studies, they sharpen his appreciation of the higher things in life. Among the arts, literature and music impress Miguel most; the former under the tutelage of Uncle Baltasar; the latter as Berenice's heritage. There is also the recurrent Gounod ballet motif to go with their relation. In his preferences, the narrator is an alter ego of the novelist.

The plot of *Los viajeros,* which supports the broader vision of the passing of an age, is simple. Miguel is lonely among his old relatives. Uncle Baltasar resents his friendship with Simón, the servants' son. He wants Miguel to be a man. He first shocks him with the presence of a naked prostitute in his greenhouse-study. But the boy soon eyes the schoolgirl Berenice and falls in love with her. She becomes for him the embodiment

---

[24] JAIME POTENCE, in *Criterio,* 28, No. 1.253 (February 9, 1956).

of beauty and purity. Her family accepts him as a descendant of the town's founder, but the girl loves him with full awareness of his ambiguous status. Baltasar objects to this relationship out of snobbishness and jealousy. He arranges for the youth to be seduced by the town whore, but Miguel will not be perverted. He keeps up with Berenice when they go to school in the city and even declines the invitation to accompany Baltasar to Europe. In the final cataclysm the uncle perishes with Berenice and Simón, barring their escape. They were looking for Miguel, who returns too late. He can only bewail his loss and keep the secret of the greenhouse key he found on Baltasar's body.

Baltasar is the central figure among the four immovable travellers. Even within the limitations of the writer's largely external characterizations, the others seem pale. There is don Fermín, a granduncle, resembling a Greco painting, who is slightly senile and who keeps buying shirts for the European tour. He warns Miguel to leave town before the final catastrophe, but he himself perishes in it. This case of foreknowledge is the only suggestion of the fantastic in what may be termed a completely romantic-realistic story.

Aunt Elisa survives the explosion but loses her mind; she still plans another itinerary when all is lost. The most normal of the lot and the least snobbish, she even taught school in town for pay and it is because of her civilizing efforts that Miguel spots Berenice. Aunt Gertrudis also survives, but goes to live a liberated life in the city, in the company of an English girl. Gertrudis, the tomboy in the family, is compared to an Amazon. She likes to simulate on horseback the continued local leadership of the family.

Baltasar is the boy's mentor but also tries to dominate him. He is another idolater, who spends his entire life on the sterile pursuit of producing a new Spanish version of the complete works of Victor Hugo. When it turns out that the uncle's verses are inferior to the nephew's, Baltasar deliberately burns his own manuscript. Miguel knows the truth and it is but one in a series of disillusionments in his rite of passage. Yet Baltasar acquaints the boy with great literature and Miguel reads not only travel guides and Hugo, but also Racine, Rimbaud, and Rilke. The uncle's sexuality is questionable; he does entertain the town whore, but it is not certain what he does with her. Some might consider his arranging the youth's loss of innocence the responsible action of a Latin father-figure bent on making a man of his ward, but the uncle may derive a vicarious satisfaction from it. His final, fatal intervention is plainly vindictive.

Simón is one of the confused adolescents who are not uncommon in early puberty but frequent in the writer's fiction. The boys used to go fishing and there was a strong attachment between them, but all changed when Berenice appeared on the scene and Simón became sullen and jealous. Berenice, too, is first seen in an in-between stage, dressed as a page of the Renaissance. She becomes a tall and slender young woman, whose winning warmth and candor is unique among the writer's creations. In his world of failures and disenchantments Berenice had to be snuffed out.

Her parents are rather stereotyped. The father is a concert pianist, who gave up the glories and risks of a world tour to marry a Creole beauty in a small town, where her father was a well-to-do coachmaker. Therefore, Angioletti is really a stranded traveller. His wife is a refined version of the Rosa of *La casa*. She is not a sex object but a nineteenth-century painting of a beauteous, kind Creole mother. The old coachmaker, a self-made bourgeois type, stands out among the lesser characters in the novel.

There are others, appearing only in episodes. The first occurs early in the book, when Miguel and Simón are challenged by Baltasar in the presence of the town whore. The boys arrive with an offering of mackerels; the whore is naked, and the uncle tells them to learn to appreciate the body of a woman. Miguel is dumbfounded, because he can conceive a nude only in terms of a Renaissance painting. At the same time a forgotten music-box is activated in the ruined greenhouse and Simón's father angrily interrupts the tableau. Later this scene seems «composed» in the narrator's memory; it becomes progressively more unreal and more like a tapestry.

More real is the ridiculous scene of his ravishment, to use Miguel's expression (*OC* V, 162). He is eighteen and, on his way home from Berenice one night, a hushed voice calls him from the old carriage house. He is silently embraced, overwhelmed, and deflowered in a vintage Peugeot, with a background of horses, chickens, an old Italian vagrant, and more ancient vehicles. The woman admits that she intercepted Miguel at Baltasar's suggestion. This shocks Miguel as much as his seeming betrayal of Berenice, as he becomes the first of a series of adolescents who are sexually initiated by experienced females in the works of Mujica Láinez.

Another disillusioning episode occurs during Aunt Duma's visit. Travelling in the company of the grotesque Prince Brandini and a French antique dealer, she is asked to stop at «Los Miradores» so that the latter might appraise its famous «Emperor's Table», a relic of Napoleon with the effigies of his marshals. (Its sale might defray the cost of the European tour.) The elderly Jewish expert —another caricature— finds the table to be a poor industrial product of the period of Napoleon III. The reader of these serio-comical pages cannot help mentally questioning the authenticity of the treasures amassed by the Saga figures and by Argentine high society in general. This seems to be writer's intent and it is expressed in Miguel's appraisal, frequently quoted, of the obsessions of all his relatives, who, in their fear of the absolute void, assume sumptuous intellectual masks and adore false idols, as did characters of *Los ídolos* and *La casa* (*OCV*, 121-24).

The satire of this class reaches its highest point in the inauguration of Aunt Ema's Charitable Foundation. The ancient lady, who had included in the project a family crypt worthy of a European dynasty, arrives, accompanied by a bishop. All known and living characters of the Saga are present in a «extraña apoteosis del linaje de la torre en llamas» (*OCV*, 211). So are the townspeople, the gauchos, and the political bosses whose «devotos... eran simultáneamente sus votos» (*OCV*, 212), and even the prostitute. There is free food and drink, but the most select guests, including the bishop, dine off Sèvres dishes depicting the most famous cocottes of the Second Empire! Compared to these festivities, the satirical treatment of the opening of an Argentine village school in Cambaceres' *Sin rumbo* (1885) seems pallid. In Mujica Láinez's book the inauguration is seen as an historical canvas of individual cartoons. It certainly does not qualify him as a representative of that oligarchy.

The scenes of *Los viajeros* are not only pictorial but in various degrees dramatic and hilarious. The author has enlivened a basically tragic tale about youthful love and the remnants of a clan with both lyricism and irony. An all-around novel with a credible plot, some suspense, and a surprise ending, it lends itself to being filmed. Its satirical aspect may have spared it the attack of the committed left. Ghiano saw in the book a turn in Mujica's novelistic development (31). A brief review in the United States noted its «subtle psychological perception».[25] Carsuzán pointed out the contrast between the clean world of Berenice and the corrupt adults of the former ruling class.[26] In spite of its favorable reception, *Los viajeros* did not reach the wide distribution of *La casa*. As a provincial tale it was, perhaps, less «central». It is also more realistic and much more satirical.

VI. «INVITADOS EN EL PARAÍSO»

Mujica Láinez did not start the last of the Saga novels until 1956. He spent ten months on it and it came out the following year. One may wonder whether it represents an afterthought. The finale of *Los viajeros* could very well be both the end of the «Flaming Tower» clan and of the Saga, but the latter, which was not chronological in the first place, was not really finished without an epilogue. *Invitados en El Paraíso,* which

---

[25] RICHARD M. MIKULSKI, *Books Abroad*, 31 (Winter 1957), 71.
[26] MARÍA EMMA CARSUZÁN, *Manuel Mujica Láinez* (Buenos Aires, 1962), p. 35. Further quotations from this book will be by author and page number in the next.

at the time of its composition almost seems contemporary, became that epilogue. Although Mujica Láinez, twenty-two years late, produced a further society novel with a novelistic time to 1942, *El gran teatro,* the novel about the guests at Villa Paradise is still an epilogue. Its characters are not society but a motley group and the villa is no paradise. The death of Duma is mentioned in conversation and decrepit Brandini just drops in.

The central character of the novel is an artist. He is modelled on the painter Victorica,[27] who had died in 1955 and was the subject of one of the writer's art books, now included in *Obras completas* V. There is something Bohemian about the world of «El Paraíso». The society of old is no more; its last authentic scion is a pregnant, unmarried intellectual, who appears late in the book and whose mésalliance provides its unbelievable, happy ending. The choice of a socially heterogeneous group for this epilogue appears deliberate. So is the choice of the narrator, an omniscient, third-person narrator, who is not distinct from the author. This makes the combination of the lyrical with the satirical a little more natural than in the last third of *Los viajeros.* It may also assuage the sexual ambivalence of the new novel. The latter aspect has, indeed, become central in Mujica Láinez's production.

The key to *Invitados en El Paraíso* may be the full-page photo in the art book *Victorica, 1884-1955,* which shows the old painter at work, with a young male model supine next to his easel: the protagonists at Villa Paradise are the spent Silvano and his youthful famulus, Kurt. Silvano has a sordid past, but his relationship with Kurt is seen as the idealized one of the old master and the adolescent companion, on a Greek or Renaissance pattern. It is a homosexual tie without any reference to homosexual acts. Both characters appear sexually ambivalent, since a forgotten episode in Silvano's heterosexual past leads to the novel's dénouement and Kurt becomes free to marry the girl, the pregnant María Lola, with whom he has fallen in love.

Silvano, whose name is significant as there is something of an old satyr about him, was born into the creole élite, but he cut all ties with it decades ago with his Bohemian life style and sexual preference. The famous artist lives in the picturesque Boca district of the capital, where he associates with sailors, fishermen, and young men of marginal status. His health is failing after many bouts of drunkenness and exploitation by Kurt's predecessors, usually vulgar youths of Italian extraction. (Mujica Láinez venerated Italian culture yet could not tolerate vulgar Italians). Silvano is so proud of his art that he does not like to dispose of his paintings. He is also quite reluctant to accept the invitation to «El Paraíso» by Tony, whom he met in a harbor bar.

---

[27] This has since been confirmed by a remark in *Páginas de Manuel Mujica Láinez* (1982), p. 140.

Kurt, too, is an outsider. The son of a Bavarian tombstone maker, a commercial sculptor, he has artistic leanings himself. He assists Silvano in his studio but is drawn more to poetry. However, unlike the two preceding novels, *Invitados* does not end on a lyrical note. In spite of his association with the ignoble world of his master, Kurt is a pure Percival — another recurring type with Mujica Láinez. He nurses the ailing painter and he enthusiastically protects the jilted María Lola. For him Villa Paradise is not an escape or a fake setting but the real thing.

«El Paraíso» is located twenty miles inland from Buenos Aires, a location different from those of the other novels. A brook separates the property from the town; it also permits swimming; and Silvano's painting «Los bañistas» becomes an important motif. The place is reached by train and the book opens on the guests' trip and late arrival at the strange, wooded place. The only link to the small town is the acquaintance of Tony's mother with the local librarian. All action takes place at «El Paraíso». The past of the characters, whether in the city or abroad, is conventionally related, without flashbacks. We are at the middle of the century; the Second World War has just ended. The time span of the novel is one of the shortest in the writer's fiction: the few weeks needed to shoot an amateur movie on Benvenuto Cellini, the subject of Tony's idolatry (and to reappear in *Bomarzo*).

This transforms the villa with its statues and broad staircase from a country home to the setting for a Renaissance film. The guests —they are all «invited»— spend some of their time as costumed actors acting out roles. Being amateurs they blunder occasionally; for instance, Pope Paul III is filmed wearing a modern wrist watch. But they take their task rather seriously, although they work with an incomplete scenario, based on Tony's novel, which —like Uncle Sebastián's— will never be completed. All this lends an unreal quality to «El Paraíso», to its strange people, and to the events there. Mujica Láinez has given a new twist to his constants of sterile pursuits, satire, and love for the cinquecento.

Tony, who divides his time between the city and the villa, can afford recreating a bit of Old Italy in a corner of Buenos Aires Province. He does it to win acceptance by the oligarchy. For he is rich and bears an old surname, but he and Tití, his mother, live on the margin of high society. His father had died soon after he was born and the mother had taken him to Europe, where he was brought up. Like the writer, he is familiar with things British, French, Italian, and even German. He caters to his mother's whims, has no worries, and his only love seems to be culture.

Tití, the mistress of the villa, is the strangest of the odd characters there. Supposedly of noble Portuguese descent, she lives in complete isolation and sallies only at night, strangely dressed, accompanied by a dalmation and a monkey. She must have been beautiful and cannot tolerate the ravages of age. She makes dramatic entries from her bedroom, stacked with votive offerings, into the great hall of the villa. The mysterious woman does not participate in the movie, but she definitely is putting on an act.

It is this mystery which constitutes the basic plot of the novel. The numerous secondary characters and their idiosyncrasies, the film-making, and the sylvan setting contribute much to the overall view of a society in transition, but they almost overshadow the limited main action. It consists of the solution of an identity problem: When Silvano and Kurt arrive and the painter first meets Tití, he knows he has seen that face before. He is quite annoyed, because he cannot remember when, where, and how he had met Tony's mother. He also feels out of place at the villa; he is afraid to lose Kurt, and he is obviously not well. He is happy only when he paints. For Kurt the extended outing has opened a whole new world of nature, swimming, acting, and female attention. When he meets María Lola, a strayed seeker after beauty, he is deeply stirred, to the chagrin of his protector.

Tití, who has feared all her life the discovery of her secret past, tries to avoid the morose Silvano. In the sixth of the seven chapters the anagnorisis occurs; the artist met her, decades ago, in a brothel downtown. He confronts Tití on her nocturnal stroll with the revelation; he is so excited that he can only stutter. She runs away, but the old painter suffers a stroke. Tití dreads the possibility of his regaining his speech, but he passes away. His death saves the «Countess» of Villa Paradise, and Kurt, with everybody's encouragement, is free to legitimize María Lola's baby.

Tití, it turns out, had been a simple Portuguese girl, whose relatives had sold her into white slavery in Buenos Aires. After three months she was rescued by a client who wanted her to live with him; she then became a chorus girl; finally a wealthy rancher took her home and even married her. Widowed soon after Tony's birth, she moved from rural Argentina to the most elegant places of Europe, where both acquired the polish expected of them back home. Their social acceptance, however, is delayed until they solve the problem of the wayward María Lola to the delight of her arch-conservative family. The visit of the girl's embarrassed sisters and pious aunt at the villa is one of the writer's better cartoons.

The black sheep in her family, María Lola had joined the radical intellectuals of the 1930s. When the anti-establishment forces, too, became conventional, she engaged in an affair with a married man, a scion of the cattle barons of old. His people persuaded him to break with his pregnant mistress. The description of this weak but physically solid man and his class is the most biting satire on part of the novelist's own background. He calls them the people

> ... que de tanto andar entre sus toros soberanos, en sus propiedades de Buenos Aires y de Entre Ríos, habían terminado por parecérseles, hasta ser las representaciones antropomorfas de esos ganados, cuyas virtudes —la buena carne, la buena sangre, el pelo lustroso, las extremidades firmes, la fecundidad y la testarudez— se habían concentrado a su vez en esos hombres rumiantes, mugientes, probos, aburridos y benévolos, y en esas mujeres monolíticas, hispánicamente honestas, con bozo y flequillo, expertas en dulces y remedios...[28]

This is only a fraction of María Lola's long story, which suffers only from a lack of paragraphing. Consecutive pages without divisions have increased in the last books, a feature which Mujica Láinez shares with many contemporary novelists.

There are further secondary personages, who are well integrated, have their own way of speaking, and are recognizable types in a no longer exclusive society. Several also use the *porteño* version of Spanish, something Mujica Láinez had not done before. However, this does not make the book a regional work nor distinct from the rest of the Saga and its universal aspects.

There is a British woman among the secondary characters, Miss Lucy, a long-term companion of Tití, former governess of Tony, an old spinster who believes both in Victorian elegance and in fairies. She even tries to catch or photograph elves on the property. This and Lucy herself are not taken too seriously, but she injects a little fantasy into a quite realistic book. (The writer's concern with the subject was to blossom later into the fairy-protagonist of his *Unicornio*.) More transcendental than fantastic is the effort of the dying Silvano to project himself into his canvas of «Los bañistas», which he confuses with the garden of his childhood. When he finally manages to bridge the gap between subject and object by entering the painting, he sees his dead body next to the sleeping Kurt. (The use of the projection motif was to be repeated by Mujica Láinez.)

Lesser characters, invited for the film, provide comic relief. There is the ripe Carlota, who has the role of Girolama Orsini —thus foreshadowing the historical Orsinis of *Bomarzo*— and who would like to sleep with Kurt. Don Boní, a remnant of the oligarchy, had seen better days but hopes to recoup by claiming the property of the Buenos Aires Zoo. He also refuses to concede his advanced age and dresses, talks, and acts like a young bachelor. With his friend, a retired police officer, who is clearly not high society, he makes an entertaining pair. Finally, Silvano's ex-lovers come to his wake.

A new social type in Mujica Láinez's fiction is Celsa, the town librarian. She is a mature spinster who smokes and keeps a diary and she is

---

[28] MANUEL MUJICA LÁINEZ, *Invitados en El Paraíso* (Buenos Aires, 1969), p. 145ff; now *OCV*, 436ff.

Tití's only contact with the outside world. Decidedly lower-class, she is visited but does not visit. She resents her exclusion by the privileged. Her diary entries wind up the novel with a would-be different viewpoint. The egalitarian Celsa erroneously sees in «El Paraíso» the last citadel of refined bluebloods who keep to themselves. For the reader, aware of their marginal status, this becomes an ironic ending.

One critic lamented the *porteño* features of the book's conversational language,[29] whereas Carsuzán praised this individualization; she also liked the democratization of society and the allusions to temporary personalities she found in the novel (44, 46, 53). Font rightly saw in «El Paraíso» both a stage and a refuge (13). Other critical observations pertaining to the Saga books equally apply to *Invitados en El Paraíso,* especially that of plot progression by a series of consecutive scenes. Yet there is a change. In Mujica Láinez's pictorial representation of characters and episodes, the former have become more cartoon-like and the latter more comedy than drama. The novel is as frivolous as the society it depicts. The futile marriage proposal of the «widowed» Bandini, ruined by the war, to the false countess of Villa Paradise represents the ultimate bankruptcy of their world. If Mujica Láinez wanted to keep portraying decadence —with both nostalgia and sarcasm— he would have to turn to other times and climes. This he did in the next phase of his writing, since he believes that human passions and failures in any elegant and picturesque setting are always the same.

---

[29] MIREYA JAIMES FREYRE, *Revista Hispánica Moderna,* 24 (1958), 337ff. She held it to be too good for a limited audience.

4

THE UNIVERSALIST PHASE

In the six books of the next phase of Mujica Láinez's production, the world rather than Buenos Aires is the stage and the novelistic time most varied. The change is marked by a gap in the writer's bibliography. He published no major work between 1957 and 1962. He was not idle, though. In addition to producing a large number of travelogues, interviews, photo-reportages, and a small art book, published in Washington,[1] Mujica was preparing his next novel, *Bomarzo,* which became his most voluminous. It fully deserved the label «Volumen gigante» in his publisher's listing. It also marks the novelist's entry among world authors, since the creator of the Saga of Buenos Aires, with which he is still associated among Hispanic readers, came to be known as «the author of *Bomarzo*», in a much broader and not exclusively literary audience.

I. «BOMARZO»

Mujica Láinez had first read about strange objects in an Italian garden in 1955. He visited the monstruous stone statues of the «Sacred Grove» of Bomarzo in 1958, during one of his many trips to the lands of the Mediterranean, and again in 1960. Before he composed the life story of the Renaissance duke who had created a grove of monsters, he thoroughly documented himself. Later, he called this procedure Flaubert-like. He conceded spending two to three years on the actual composition of the novel's six hundred and seventy pages; he also defended his right to «internationalize» his themes.

In spite of its size, the 1962 book became one of the writer's best-selling works. Within a year it won the National Literary Prize. In 1964 it was awarded the Kennedy Prize and it inspired the text of a Cantata,[2] with music by Alberto Ginastera, which was performed first in Washington,

---

[1] *Argentina* (Pan American Union, 1961).
[2] Available only in *Páginas de Manuel Mujica Láinez,* a 1982 anthology.

D.C. The Cantata, grown into an opera with a poetic libretto by Mujica Láinez, likewise was first staged in the United States (1967). The opera's success and subsequent prohibition by the authorities in Buenos Aires only added to the sales of the novel. The latter's Italian version had appeared in 1965. It had an American version in 1969, a British one in 1970 —both in the highly praised translation by Rabassa— and a German one in 1971. The first of several editions in Spain came out in 1975. By 1972 the Argentine authorities had relented and the opera was finally shown in the fatherland of the composer and the librettist.

Whereas the opera, whose text will be treated briefly as a separate item, is an effective, compact work, the novel about a creator of monsters is itself a monstrosity. It has been called fatiguing and its prose overloaded.[3] Font considers its content «sofocante, macabro y repelente» (123). What is it that caused its success and what are its literary merits? It is, above all, a tour de force. Although steeped in history, it is not novelized history. It does not even pretend to be an historical novel. (Ghiano felt that the writer had not skirted the pitfalls of that genre, in which the framework drowns out the characters. He also noted that Mujica Láinez had merely transferred to the Renaissance his habitual obsessions [16].) *Bomarzo* purports to be the real autobiography of a lesser sixteenth-century prince, reincarnated, in twentieth-century Buenos Aires, in the writer. The latter declared that he remembered his earlier existence, when he sensed the stone monsters of the Sacred Grove to be an allegorical biography of the Duke.

Mujica Láinez completely identified himself with Pier Francesco Orsini. The dedication page and the last page of the book[4] clearly show that writer, narrator, and character are the same person. Although I have noted Mujica's propensity to unusual characters, the combination is not just another device. The writer's discovery «He is I» is equally «I am he», the fictional projection of his ego into the sixteenth-century. Therefore, the Duke of Bomarzo is pure (fact and fancy) Mujica Láinez, and the book, albeit quite different from his earlier works, contains the usual elements of his writing. The real Duke can be traced in all kinds of archives. According to an art historian, his rock statues may, indeed, reflect life experiences and foreign influences.[5] Yet to see in those sculptures the

---

[3] CARMELINA DE CASTELLANOS, *Tres nombres en la novela argentina* (Santa Fe, 1967), p. 24. The author himself quipped «yo no lo he vuelto a leer nunca», in *El mundo de Manuel Mujica Láinez. Conversaciones con María Esther Vázquez* (Buenos Aires, 1983), p. 96. This source will be cited as *Mundo* by page number in the text.

[4] MANUEL MUJICA LÁINEZ, *Bomarzo* (Buenos Aires, 1968). This book, too, will be cited by pages number in the text.

[5] JOSEPHINE VON HENNEBERG, «Bomarzo: nuovi dati e un'interpretazione», *Storia dell'Arte*, 13 (1972), 43-55; also, «Bomarzo: The Extravagant Garden of Pier Francesco Orsini», *Italian Quarterly*, 11, No. 42 (1967), 3-19.

creations of a monstrous mind, anxious to perpetuate his monstrous life story, is plain and, obviously, good fiction.

The metempsychosis of Pier Francesco Orsini into Manuel Mujica Láinez —which would have delighted the Modernists of yore— enables the reader to view the pageant of the Duke's life with a modern detachment and the psychological and critical knowledge of our time. But it also made the protagonist a man with a variety of complexes. He is a limping hunchback, sporadically impotent, with bisexual and criminal tendencies — and a much more interesting novelistic character than the healthy warrior with minor literary inclinations that the real Pier Francesco seems to have been.[6] Also, let us not forget that the novel claims to be a confession of a man who lived in a turbulent age of both great splendor and decay, all facts which contributed to the book's success.

Although there is much plotting in the novel, as one can expect, including historical conspiracies, one can hardly call Pier Francesco's life story a plot. He is born with an astrological prediction of immortality, but, as the deformed second son of a condottiere of illustrious lineage, he suffers discrimination and traumas. As an adolescent he spends some time at the Medici court. Since he does not prevent his older brother's accidental death, he himself becomes the Duke. He engages in sexual orgies and black magic. He marries the beautiful niece of a future Pope, but cannot consummate the bond until he arranges for his wife to be seduced by his younger brother; whereupon he has him killed. He surrounds himself with antiques, art objects, and intellectuals — some of historical fame. He ingloriously participates in wars in France and witnesses the battle of Lepanto from a deck chair. After the death of his first wife, he remarries for money, but concentrates his final efforts on attaining glory and eternal life. He gains the former by creating the most unusual rock sculptures near his castle north of Rome, but he loses his life when his nephew —to avenge his father's murder— adds poison to the newly discovered immortality potion.

All this truculence is being justified as typical of the epoch and it may very well be, but it is the temporal and spatial setting which prevents the book from becoming merely the morbid exploration of a tortured protagonist. The Venice of the Doges, the Florence of the Medicis, the Rome of the Renaissance Popes, the artists and the writers of the period, even the battles —related in the writer's «I was there» fashion— are much more than background for the deeds and misdeeds of the Duke of Bomarzo.

---

[6] Letter from Professor Henneberg to George O. Schanzer, dated 10 October 1974.

His is the only viewpoint expressed and the countless other characters, whose number may exceed even those of the Saga of Buenos Aires, are seen through him. He is quite unreliable and Font's detailed analysis points out the Duke's insincerity (121ff). His presentation of life in Renaissance Italy equally serves to impress the reader and to seduce innocent youths at his time. He is endowed with a certain omniscience, since he can scrutinize the recesses of his own mind in the light of Freud (named), Adler and Jung (unnamed), and his twentieth-century experience. (The composer of the opera version even saw in Pier Francesco a modern anti-hero.) The other characters, the Orsini, Farnese, and Medici clans, the scholars, writers, painters, and sculptors; Cellini, Aretino, and many more, are not fully developed and their portrayal may only be partially accurate. But Pier Francesco insists on the superiority of *his* experience over historical and documentary evidence.

In the opera version the multitude of characters is reduced to twelve singers, a few supernumeraries, and a chorus. Using the dramatic qualities of the subject, Mujica Láinez produced a well-structured libretto. It is quite appropriate, therefore, to compare the two forms. The novel is written in eleven chapters, which contain an even larger number of incidents and animated tableaux, all in linear sequence. The opera consists of fifteen key scenes in the life of Pier Francesco; it both opens and concludes with the death scene in the infernal grotto. Then his life experiences are shown in consecutive flashbacks. The important dream passages of the novel, which are highly erotic, become ballet sequences. These dance scenes —which are supposed to be performed topless and appear to be artistically justified— were found to be contrary to public morals in Argentina. Basically, the libretto is much more tame than the book. Therefore, the censors, by cancelling the Teatro Colón debut with an international cast, only drew attention to a novel which harps on masturbation, transvestism, pederasty, and quite unambiguous bisexuality. As a matter of fact, Mujica Láinez has been accused of proselitizing for his preference. The lustiness and depravity of the period, with which the narrator justifies his actions, was, to be sure, the choice of the novelist.

The opera text is written nearly all in verse, mainly the traditional Hispanic eight- and eleven-syllable lines, with assonance. Their lyricism facilitated the composer's task, even if he used quite a modern musical idiom. The opening and closing song of the shepherd boy —merely alluded to on page six hundred and sixty-seven of the novel— which contrasts his innocence with the tortuous life of the Duke, and the choral passages show that Mujica Láinez can be a dramatic poet. The theatrical economy of the opera also includes a reappearance of the grandmother's voice, a combination of characters and extension of their lives. The libretto, of course, lacks the erudite, cultural wealth of the dense novel, with its long periods and paragraphs and, at times, tedious prose.

In a few instances the prose is quite poetic and the novel has also some good dialogues. In general, the omission of some episodes would have greatly improved the book. (It seems good fiction that the protagonist is armed a knight by Charles V and that he meets a Spanish soldier named Cervantes on the eve of the battle of Lepanto, but details of the plight of Julia Gonzaga are quite unessential.) Also, enumerations appear excessive, even if name calling and repetitions in the Mujica Láinez manner serve the purpose of recapitulating and reinforcing: e.g. the myth of the Orsini clan, with its catalogue of heroes, saints, and sinners under their totemistic she-bear figure.

There are other motifs and techniques which are recurrent with the writer: the decadence and even threatening bankruptcy of the descendants of illustrious ancestors (accompanied, as with the Modernists, by disdainful remarks about merchants) and frequent, strange re-encounters: e.g. the ascetic Spaniard of Orsini's youth re-emerges as a Jesuit at Lepanto time, and the great courtesan Pantasilea actually joins the Orsini family in Chapter X. (Her pompous wedding becomes a parody —another of Mujica's favorite techniques— of the Duke's wedding to Julia Farnese.) There are allusions to the novelist's other works and preoccupations: the Unicorn, the Labyrinth, and the Minotaur who requires the sacrifice of youths of both sexes. We also find the importance of the works of great authors in *Bomarzo*, such as Ariosto[7] and Garcilaso de la Vega. The novel has its share of Jews (in the episode of the translation of arcane manuscripts) and of a catastrophic fire (in the destruction of the alchemist's den). There are ephebic twins, a strong sexy woman, and a great old lady, Diana Orsino, who seems to be patterned after the writer's remarkable grandmother.[8]

The Duke is a great collector; luxurious, heterogeneous, or mysterious objects are very important in the book. The stone monsters of the Sacred Grove, e.g. the Turtle or the Elephant, do not speak but they tell a story. With the novel's Renaissance setting, the emphasis on the pictorial and the sculptural can be expected; yet the entire book seems a series of famous paintings. For Cruz it is the peak of Mujica Láinez's pictorial technique (123). One recognizes the Coronation of Charles V or the Procession of the Sacrament Mounted on a Mule, but there must be many

---

[7] The book's links to Ariosto, Cellini, and others are shown in ALMA NOVELLA MARANI's «El renacimiento en Manuel Mujica Láinez», *Studi di letteratura ispano-americana* (1981), 45-71. Università degli Studi di Venezia, No. 11.
[8] Traces of Justa Varela appear in a number of works of Mujica Láinez. In the dedication of my copy of *Bomarzo* he calls it the novel «en la que puse mucho de mi vida anterior e interior».

other canvasses, real or apocryphal. Pier Francesco even insists that the Portrait of an Unknown Noble, by Lorenzo Lotto, is his own portrait, minus the hump. Julia has a Ghirlandaio-type neck; other characters are compared to frescos or friezes. Even near death the Duke is aware of the artistic effect of the scene: «Componíamos una estampa fabulosa, una ilustración para uno de esos libros mágicos...» (666).

Serious but not devoid of humor is the anachronism of Orsini's twentieth-century perspective. He uses words and terms in various languages and scholarly jargons; he has foreknowledge of events and of locations of objects long after his death; he loves to surround himself with «intelectuales».

Mujica Láinez's deliberate espousal of anachronism is part of the truculent book's increasing irony. The death of the «immortal» Duke is, of course, ironic; so is the conversion of a horrible skeleton, found in a secret closet, into an object of public veneration in the local parish church; so too is the metamorphosis of a gipsy woman's rags, which facilitated Pier Francesco's escape after defeat in Flanders, into victorious banners. There are also grotesque scenes, such as the wedding banquet and, later, the parody of the whole ceremony. The novelist has become sarcastic. He calls the condottieri traffickers of death; he observes that the future founder of Buenos Aires, at the Emperor's coronation, displays syphilitic sores; and when Pantasilea joins the family, he calls her a retired whore. When the cardinal, the Duke's uncle, dies, he comments: «cien servidores proclamaban con ceremoniosa pereza el esplendor de su jerarquía y el desorden de sus finanzas» (399).

As we have seen, the world view reflected in Mujica Láinez's big novel is a rather negative one. It is *not* a glorification of the Renaissance. (As a matter of fact, the Duke alludes to baroque elements and his statues are definitely transitional. Late in life, on the other hand, he seeks a medieval spirit of repentance.) He experiences one disillusion after the other. Finally, instead of eternal life, he merely attains reincarnation in an Argentine novelist who wins for him a precarious literary immortality.[9] We note the constant suggestion that truth itself is elusive, that problems and conflicts can be resolved only aesthetically, and that man can transcend himself only by artistic creativity.

There is much of the occult, of satanism, and of alchemy in *Bomarzo*, but their use in Pier Francesco's quest is not shown to be successful; nor are these elements new with Mujica Láinez. I do not consider their inclusion an evolution to Magic Realism.[10]

---

[9] The writer claims that among the townspeople of Bomarzo and others it is his version of the Duke which has become the authentic one.

[10] Cf. ANITA WAGMAN's unpublished dissertation «Historical Vision and Magic Realism in the Works of Manuel Mujica Láinez», Michigan State University, 1977.

Criticism of the novel ranged from enthusiastic to mildly critical. In addition to comments already cited, the following seem appropriate: David Foster found the book not great but one of the most memorable in recent Argentine literature.[11] Borges called the novel a real contribution to the genre.[12] Without clearly explaining his contention, Rojas Guardia held that *Bomarzo* prefigured the ambience of *Cien años de soledad*,[13] the all-time Latin American best-seller. The explanation may be Villena's idea that *Bomarzo* shows a clear use of «*fusión mítica* (es decir, la historia se refiere a un hoy casi intemporal)» (26). I consider the novel remarkable but not superior to *La casa,* which is of one piece.

II. «EL UNICORNIO»

There have been questions as to which period *Bomarzo* is to represent: one of Mujica Láinez' fellow academicians called it a baroque novel about a Renaissance prince, and a Spanish critic ascribed its monstrous figures, their creator, and the novelistic treatment of his life to the transitional style known as «manierismo».[14] Mujica's second historical novel, *El unicornio,* clearly represents the French Middle Ages; furthermore the Latin Kingdom of Jerusalem, the setting of nearly half the book, is a creation of French knights. In choosing great moments for his novelistic triptych, the writer picked the twelfth century for novel number two.

He seems to have conceived the idea on a journey to the Near East in 1960, but he did not carry it out until after *Bomarzo* was completed. From 1962 to 1965, the year *El unicornio* came out, the writer only published poems related to Shakespeare[15] and a translation of a French play.[16] His new novel required as careful a documentation as the one laid in sixteenth-century Italy.

The two works have much in common, but Mujica Láinez did not follow a set pattern in elaborating his historically-based novels. Rather one could speak of evolutionary changes. Each book is more human and humorous than the preceding one. Thus, *El unicornio* is much less grim than *Bomarzo*. It is also more lyrical and, above all, more compact. Not only are its three hundred and eighty-eight pages, in nine chapters, less

---

[11] DAVID WILLIAM FOSTER, «The Monstrous in Two Argentine Novels», *Americas,* 24, No. 2 (1972), 33.
[12] Cited on the book's back cover.
[13] PABLO ROJAS GUARDIA, *La realidad mágica* (Caracas, 1969), p. 37.
[14] JORGE CAMPOS, «Bomarzo, novela manierista», *Insula,* 292 (1971), 11.
[15] *Cincuenta sonetos de Shakespeare,* tr. by Mujica Láinez (Buenos Aires, 1963). Poem «A Shakespeare», *La Nación,* 19 April 1964. Article, «La amistad de Shakespeare», *Sur,* 289-90 (1964), 30-33.
[16] MOLIÈRE'S *Las mujeres sabias (Les Femmes savantes),* tr. by Manuel Mujica Láinez (Buenos Aires, 1964). This version was performed by the Comedia Nacional.

dense, but also the writer made no effort to encompass a whole period in a colossal canvas. Instead, he presented «una visión personalísima de la Edad Media», as stated on the book's rear cover, and a «succession of scenes (tableaux) of constant irony», as he told me, in English, by letter.[17] *El unicornio* seemed to be a favorite of his and he frequently alluded to it in interviews. Mujica Láinez deplored its initial mere average success and he was delighted when the novel was reissued in Spain by Planeta in a series of «Grandes Novelistas Hispánicos». Recently an English version has been published in Canada (1982), England (1983), and the United States (1983), translated by Mary Fitton, with a Foreword by Borges.

El unicornio, like its predecessor, has an immortal narrator. This affords both a period eye-witness and a modern perspective. But the novel presents itself as the memoirs of a dramatized narrator distinct from the writer, whose idiosyncrasies she merely shares. This time the narrator is not an historical figure but one that derives a sort of authenticity from art and literature. The fairy Melusina is Mujica Láinez's most unusual personage. She is a female narrator, she is truly fabulous, she is a re-elaboration, and she cannot die. This made it possible for the writer to incorporate the whole world of fantasy and to project reality from an «unreal» viewpoint. It also enabled him to appropriate a large body of Old French and Provençal literature. And he could portray the attraction of male beauty without choosing a homosexual protagonist. Finally, since all this is done with tongue-in-cheek, he could convey the idea that immortality might be a burden or a punishment rather than a goal. Melusina is chatty, sexy; she seems quite sincere and readers found her very «simpática», perhaps the writer's nicest creation. The fact is that this fairy is deeply human. Her memoirs are full of frustrations, especially in her love for a mortal whose life can be said to constitute the plot.

Melusina is taken from a miniature in the famous *Book of Hours* of the Duke of Berry. She records her romance, writing in the tower of the French castle of Lussignan. A widow for centuries, she falls in love with a beautiful adolescent, who resembles her late husband. Aiol really is one of her descendants, the illegitimate son of an impoverished veteran of the crusades. His mother is a former prostitute, married to an artisan who is working on a basilica in Poitiers. Melusina, who is invisible (and, therefore, has the problems of communication and alienation of modern characters) has to contend with many rivals, since Aiol's beauty —which almost seems a curse— arouses all, of both sexes. First he stirs his boyish step-sister Azelaís, of unknown father, who has an incestuous fixation on him. Melusina follows the still chaste youth, his aging father, and a group of errant players (who suggest the origin of the theater) to Poitiers.

---

[17] Letter to George O. Schanzer, dated 25 September 1972.

There Azelaís, in vain, tries to seduce Aiol, whereupon she has a passionate fit —with a suggestion of masturbation— which is interpreted as demoniac possession by the townspeople. During the rites of exorcism, her stepfather, the stone craftsman, accidentally falls to his death. Aiol and Ozil, the old knight, feel guilty and spend a chaste chapter with the hermit St. Brendan in the magic forest of Lussac, in the company of fantastic creatures. With the invisible fairy they then move to the unchaste Provençal castle of Seramunda. (There is a constant see-saw of sin and penance in the book, as well as a very Modernist allegory of dualism; e.g. the unicorn, which Aiol inherits, is both a symbol of purity and of impurity.)

Deflowered by Seramunda in a grotesque bath scene, the lad is saved from the desire —and the wrath— of the lady's pervert husband by a complicated substitution intrigue, in which Seramunda's long-time troubadour is killed. When that courtly poet's heart is served to Seramunda at a banquet, she jumps to her death. After this well-known and dramatic episode Aiol and his father return to the forest, only to meet the hermit's magic funeral procession. They also encounter Azelaís and an ex-actor. Ozil is killed at the next tournament, but Aiol is armed a knight by the dead man's sword. After the celebration to follow he sleeps with his sister, who then disappears. To atone for his sin Aiol vows to go to the Holy Land to fight the infidel and to recover the long-lost heirloom of the Sacred Lance which pierced Christ.

He does not go alone, for Melusina, who, for obvious reasons, sought a body, is granted her wish, but her fairy-mother makes her male, the young knight Melusin. As such she accompanies her beloved to Palestine, a pilgrimage not without homosexual and bisexual overtones. In the Near East, the Frankish kingdom, headed by a leprous boy king, is tottering from internal intrigues and the onslaughts of Saladin. The protagonists —and the reader— are exposed to a lot of history, in dynastic and ecclesiastic squabbles, but also to much oriental luxury and depravity. The ex-fairy is seduced by the mother of the king and Aiol has a spell of heterosexual excesses. Melusin(a) then reverts to her magic self, protected by King Oberon who lends her his magic horn. (The latter provides air-rescues at critical moments.) When the leper king dies, his mysterious nurse turns out to be the repentant, leprous, and dying Azelaís. This book of adventures —the narrator calls it thus— ends when Aiol, on a hint from the Wandering Jew, finds the Sacred Lance, conveniently tagged. However, sexually harrassed by a prelate's deranged mistress, he jumps into an abyss in the ruins of Jordanian Petra. The departing Melusina then sees the «Knight of the Lance» and other key characters in a cloud, in a sort of Christian apotheosis, which recalls the poetic finales of Mujica Láinez's gauchesque biographies.

The foregoing outline has sketched action, characters, setting, motifs, and techniques of *El unicornio*. Obviously, many of them are recurrent with the novelist. The action is somewhat reduced in the oriental portion, where we find a display, excessive at times, of historical and archeological erudition with sumptuous, quite Modernist, descriptions of objects and scenes. The characters are only two; in fact only one and a half, because even Aiol is seen from the outside, when Melusina's omniscience is curtailed by her becoming Melusin. All others are more like figures in a ballet.

Among the motifs religion stands out. No wonder it is stronger in this medieval romance than in any other work of Mujica Láinez. But is either decorative, as it was with the Modernists, or the butt of his ironic vision, or both. The book is full of hieratic ceremonies, processions, and rites, as well as allusions to commercialized feasts, corrupt clerics, and rich vestments — adorned with Arabic quotations from the Koran. The writer's deliberate irreverence includes even the listing of the Holy Foreskin in the enumeration of relics.

The most striking technical advancement is Mujica's unabashed recycling of great literature and art. This involves retelling of known French works and large-scale re-enactment of scenes from paintings, sculpture, mosaics, and miniatures. Melusina is a miniature brought to life and, as a self-conscious narrator, she even concedes she is recreating. Her «How to catch a unicorn» is quite charming. The account of the characters visiting the existing tomb of Seramunda has something Cervantine about it. But literature is not only an inspiration and incorporated, sometimes with authors cited —both of the period and later days— it is also satirized; e.g. the fairy says «Hace aquí su entrada el santo ermitaño que invariablemente figura en estas narraciones».[18] She is also aware that she is part of an allegory (382). All this is connected, of course, with the book's encompassing irony, in spite of all the mystical and magical apparatus used by the novelist. He does not expect us to take quite seriously the fairy's sex change, her second loss of virginity, melodramatic screams, and magic horn tooting.

Mujica Láinez made no attempt to «recreate» the Middle Ages. In a recent interview he conceded that he could not vouch for their being as shown in *El unicornio*.[19] He wanted to make the latter the second part of a «tríptico» of «anti-history», as he called it in the aforementioned letter. This is why he could describe courtly love lyric as «flirt poético» (133), would picture snacks that accompany tournaments, the decadence of chivalrous squander and oriental lavishness, and, in general, the unholy

---

[18] MANUEL MUJICA LÁINEZ, *El unicornio* (Buenos Aires, 1965), p. 114. Further quotations by page number in the text.
[19] Interview with María Sáenz Quesada, *Clarín*, 10 January 1980.

and unheroic aspects of a great age. It certainly is a reflection of his concept of the persistence of human passions: humanity was the same then as it is now; people are made «con el mismo limo» (135). They have both a bit of an angel and the devil. «El hombre... es siempre el mismo, en todas las épocas» (311). Life is a succession of deaths. Victory is followed by defeat. Lovemaking is not always fun. Indeed, «todo gran amor es imposible y en eso finca su grandeza» (270). But this melancholy outlook is paired with a tolerant smile and an enormous aesthetic comprehension.

Not all the critics caught the irony of Mujica Láinez's «medieval» novel. Cruz rightly saw in it an attempt to demythify history (131). Font stressed its Cervantine aspects (16). Villena noted the mythic fusion of its fantastic elements (27). Wagman, however, considered these elements a progression towards Magic Realism, forgetting that the latter is serious and Mujica Láinez is not. One reviewer completely missed the ironic treatment of history, finding the story lacked «probability» and did not convey the impression of greatness. He expressed the hope that Mujica Láinez would return to testimonial literature.[20] As an historical linguist, Lerner even objected to the book's anachronisms, archaisms, neologisms, and faulty constructions, all features which are patently deliberate.

After *El unicornio,* which I consider a better novel than *Bomarzo,* Mujica Láinez did not rid himself of pseudo-history, escapist fancy, and banality, as Lerner had recommended. Rather, he wholeheartedly embraced them to satirize. What had been an ever-increasing aspect of his work became the keynote of the next four books.

III. «Crónicas reales»

The writer delayed completion of the planned novelist triptych, which, after all, had a basic serious intent. He turned again to the hybrid genre of linked tales and, in 1966, he wrote *Crónicas reales,* whose dominant and constant tone is one of levity. It required no documentation and he wrote it in a little more than three months. He admitted he had fun doing it, i.e. making fun of hoary European traditions. The slim volume —its approximately eighty thousand words are half of *El unicornio* and less than a third of *Bomarzo*— came out the following year. In the same period Mujica Láinez also produced an edition of writings by a compatriot, two stories, and a recorded autobiography. Two translations of foreign plays remain unpublished.[21]

[20] Isaías Lerner, «Manuel Mujica Láinez, *El unicornio*», *Revista Iberoamericana,* 33 (1967), 165-67.
[21] *Oscar Hermes Villordo* (Buenos Aires, 1966). «Amanecer», *Estafeta Literaria,* 381-82 (1967). «La larga cabellera negra», of 1967, eventually included in *El*

Crónicas reales is composed of eleven episodes from the history of an imaginary Eastern European country, spanning the centuries from the early Middle Ages to a «now». The sequence is chronological, but it is not a systematic history. The episodes can be read as independent items of short fiction; as a matter of fact, Villena included one complete section in his anthology; another appeared in a 1981 collection. What holds them together is the protagonists' connection with the same eccentric dynasty. Also, the writer used some «tacks» to interrelate the tales and an epilogue (Chapter XII) recapitulates would-be great moments in the country's history in a sort of guided tour. There are even allusions to details of past and not-yet-written works by Mujica Láinez; e.g. the first king descends from a fairy.

The characters are all recognizable archetypes of human foibles; history lovers will enjoy identifying specific great personages or combinations thereof, poetically caricaturized. The tales are of varied length (ranging from about four to twelve thousand words) and of much more even quality than those of *Misteriosa Buenos Aires*. Two or three are among the writer's best items of short fiction.

The gallery of personages is opened by the liberator of the country and founder of the dynasty. A stone mason, he causes the new cathedral to collapse over the ruling, lecherous robber baron. He marries the latter's mannish sister and takes over. Next is their incredibly —and inconveniently— holy son, St. Eximio, who vows perpetual nudity, attracts fallen women, and, unfortunately, also his sister-in-law, the queen. The following ruler loves alchemy and, with helpers from the ghetto, constructs a number of mysterious, useless gadgets, which the reader recognizes as the prototypal sewing machine, the flush toilet, and the record player. Having no off-spring he builds a robot who governs after his death. The tale ends when the queen gives birth to a little automaton beyond repair.

Next is a king who loves rope-dancing and can balance everything, including foreign politics and internal finances. This tale is followed by one on the Immortal Lovers. A prince and his not-quite-princely bride are killed during the wedding procession, skewered by one arrow from the wicked, rank-conscious queen. Obviously, the victims, as the previous and following personages, become part of the country's legendary patrimony.

To the Age of Discovery belongs the (illegitimate) Navigator. With three adventurers and a crew of madmen he accidentally encounters the hairy queen of savages. They have to sleep with her before she guides them to the Fountains of Youth and Wisdom. After they drink from these

brazalete (1978). Record «Manuel Mujica Láinez por él mismo», AMB Discográfica (1967). Translations from Marivaux and Shakespeare.

springs, the travellers return as erudite children, whose revolutionary ideas have to be eliminated with them. Then we have a clash between a king and his younger, foppish brother, representing, respectively, Eastern theocratic and Western corrupting tendencies. The conflict ends when the King to be murdered dies a natural death and the Italian mercenary killers crush the fop that hired them.

Progress cannot be stopped and the next monarch sacrifices himself to be up-to-date by attending an orgy. Instead of being seduced by a boy, he awakens with a beautiful girl, who becomes the Royal Favorite and advances the country culturally. She even wins an important battle by a heroic strip-tease. The following tale concerns a princess, whose salon unites real celebrities from Wagner to Rilke. When she realizes that her late husband, a celebrated hunter, had chased women rather than game, she is upset and joins a hippy poet's group; in a back-to-nature mood she permits the scuttling of her famous cameo collection and jumps to her death.

In the twentieth century we meet an elderly count, who lives in a run-down castle, rented to produce a British vampire film. The movie people do not realize that he is a real vampire, until he is killed, with the help of magic, by the jealous spinster script-writer. Then the monarchy is replaced by a leftist regime, which tolerates the presence of a slightly mad dowager queen. When the dynasty is swept back into power, the Forgotten Queen takes over. It is implied that this senile ruler and the robot were the best the country ever had.

It is the final chapter, based on apocryphal sources, which summarizes the great past of this nation of uncertain geography. (The Germanic/Slavic roots are obvious, but hints of Romance and Byzantine influences abound.) The process of mythmaking becomes one of demythologization, as the previous ironic third-person narrator is revealed as the author of the guide to the palaces, art treasures, and souvenirs of the House of Hercules and von Orbs. This brochure-chapter is written in the majestic first person plural in a turgid, patriotic prose, interspersed with prosaic references to admissions, postcards, and restrooms. Behind that unctuous writer, supposedly an art historian and academician aspiring to promotion, Cruz imagines his chuckling colleague Mujica Láinez (140). He even inserts himself into one of the plots as the Shakespearean scholar who was to accompany the king to the orgy, wearing a Shakespeare ring, a possession of Mujica.

The naughty *Crónicas reales* are well served by its author's penchant for episodic structure. The episodes are likely to be quite dramatic and, in this book of corrosive irony, the scenes tend to be grotesque. One need only to visualize the birth of the baby robot or the return of the discoverers as learned infants. It shows that many aspects of the writer's technique, themes, and motifs —serious before or with a veiled irony— are now openly comical. This includes even such weighty issues as the problem of historic truth and of the extension of life. Likewise the use of the fantastic and of magic, the whole «La jurisdicción de los fantasmas» (the title of the final Chapter XII), is funny. The familiar motifs of tapestry weaving, of the aggressive woman, of nudity, of the sudden scream, even objects have become risible. Sex, in *Crónicas reales,* tends to be more normal but also more frivolous.

Nothing, indeed, escaped being the butt of Mujica Láinez's satire. The outline above indicates that he makes fun of genealogy, hagiography, technology, bureaucracy, erudition, national idiosyncrasies, chauvinism, politics, the maffia, film making, art and literary criticism, too many to exemplify. Let two samples suffice, from areas not yet pointed out: Mujica Láinez mocks spying when he provides the Austrian ambassador's confidential report on the king's mistress. When her statue is destroyed and only her breasts are preserved in the national museum, he attributes to paleontology the know-how to reconstruct her body.

All this shows that the writer availed himself of all the standard techniques of satire, including puns (most of which are untranslatable), plays on words, exaggeration, repetition, contrast, and, above all, funny names. The nature poet who converts the sophisticated princess is called Phalo Doro; the once Forgotten Queen belongs to the House of Tram and Taxis. Mujica Láinez also borrows known lines from famous writers, e.g. Darío's «Marcha triunfal» verses for his restoration parade.[22] Throughout the book he makes much use of chaotic enumeration. Some of these lists recall passages from the pen of García Márquez: a collection of urinals and the stress on oblivion appear both in the latter's *Cien años de soledad* and Mujica's *Crónicas,* published in the same year. Deliberately comical seem also the extensive adjectivation, especially in the uncommon Spanish pre-position, as in the Forgotten Queen's audiences (288), and verbs opening clauses, e.g. in the effects of the vampire feeding on his victims (261).

The most clever satire is found in the tenth of the tales of the entertaining volume. Mujica Láinez himself considers the Vampire story one of his best.[23] It should be noted that it appeared before Cortázar used the topic in *62 Modelo para armar* and also prior to both a serious work about Dracula and couple of satirical films on the theme. «The Vampire» of *Crónicas reales* is also very interesting structurally. It ironically confuses various levels of reality, from the outermost, the country's history, to

---

[22] MANUEL MUJICA LÁINEZ, *Crónicas reales* (Buenos Aires, 1967), p. 288. Quotation by page number in the text.
[23] Letter to George O. Schanzer, dated 24 March 1973. See also my study «Un caso de vampirismo satírico: Mujica Láinez», *Otros mundos, otros fuegos* (East Lansing, MI, 1975). XVI Congreso Internacional de Literatura Iberoamericana.

the innermost, the film «The Beast of Wurzburg», shot at the supposedly real Wurzburg castle. In the tale of the eerie Count Zappo, he himself is hired to star in a fictitious script, composed by a writer of Gothic fiction. There is constant conflict over the questions of art/fiction versus reality and the superiority of one or the other. The height of hilarity is reached when the real vampire is taught to act himself by Lupo Belosi, veteran of horror movies, and the authentic ambience is filled with fake props. Since Zappo draws blood from all women but the aged Miss Brady, she jealously enters the plot of her own script and uses a potion and magic to defeat the monster. The killing is filmed but the news is suppressed by the government.[24]

Crónicas reales may have had more success with the critics than with the public. (It did win a prize in 1968.) Villena found the book's ironic fantasy more humorous than the satires of Swift (23ff). One Argentine commentator called Mujica's tales «la quintaesencia del espíritu sagaz y erudito, ágil, irónico y sensual de este gran narrador».[25] For me, *Crónicas reales* is the best of the writer's books of linked stories. He himself clearly enjoyed the evolution his fiction had undergone and he proceeded to write more in the new vein.

IV. «DE MILAGROS Y DE MELANCOLÍAS»

Mujica Láinez's next book was to do for South America what the preceding one had done for the Old World, i.e. create an anti-history in a historical sequence.[26] *De milagros y de melancolías* was written in six and a half months, twice the time it took to compose *Crónicas reales*, and was twice its size. It was published in 1969. Its six chapters, followed by an Epilogue and an imaginary Bibliography, are much less independent than the tales of the previous work; they afford a sort of comprehensive, albeit episodic history of a locality. Therefore, the book is generally considered a novel or, one might say, a novel in the form of history to satirize history.

The locality is again an imaginary one, the city of San Francisco de Apricotina del Milagro. This provincial capital is the archetypical Latin American town and its history is the paradigm of the development of Spanish America, from its founding to a present of tyranny. A «Epílogo espiritista» permits even a glimpse into the future or a re-start, a new feature among the writer's coordinates. The archetypical city is a synthe-

---

[24] «El vampiro» was reprinted in *El poeta perdido y otros relatos* (Buenos Aires, 1981).
[25] ENRIQUE REVOL, «La tradición fantástica en la literatura argentina», *Revista de Estudios Hispánicos*, 2 (1968), 21f.
[26] According to the author's letter cited in note 17 above.

tic one with an equally synthetic geography. Yet the book is written, supposedly, in Buenos Aires, by an exiled historian, who bases his great chronicle of the fortunes and misfortunes of San Francisco de Apricotina on a wide range of apocryphal sources, scholarly or otherwise.

Apocryphal is also the epigraph, cited from the account of one of the discoverers, who compared the fate of the city to a «rosario de milagros y de melancolías» — which explains the title of the book. This funny novel on a sad topic does not allude specifically to Argentina but to a universalized Latin America. The cultured, cosmopolitan Argentina is not mocked in it; the other —the violent, primitive, and vulgar Argentina— is.

The book opens with the arrival of the conquerors, the bedraggled band led by Nufrio de Bracamonte, in their vain quest for El Dorado — another of the writer's constants. Their aged, syphilitic leader has a picaresque background; the others, too, are archetypes of the period: the saintly friar, the poor-proud noble, the fat Indian mistress, the soldier-chronicler, etc. In the name of greedy and corrupt officials they found a new settlement on a spot of wondrous events which they consider miraculous. After the death of Nufrio, the one-eyed Founder, his son Baltasar is recalled to the mother-country, in chains. I hardly need to continue, as this is not a plot; it is history; yet what matters is the way it is told as a parody: from the Spaniards' humble beginnings as goatherds, through the Indian ex-madam's finding a crude fertility idol —which becomes a center of Marian devotion— to the unending trial of Baltasar, represented by a Barón Kafka.

With personages subordinated to a satirical technique, there is an almost total lack of characterization (which was never the writer's forte). Therefore, after the unglorious beginnings, the city of portents experiences a rather dull colonial era, under oddly-named governors of uncertain number who are lightly sketched as venal, lecherous, monomaniacal or plainly foolish. Among them Mujica Láinez sneaked in a man with literary leanings, who wrote a play on a hunchback, which was forbidden by the bishop and the mayor. This Don Laín Láinez y Veintelibros is remembered, whereas his censors are forgotten. Thus the novelist followed his practice of including himself in the text.

The archetype of the Liberator is a composite of that figure as seen in Latin American schoolbooks. The rebellious son of a Spanish bureaucrat and tax maniac, he frees the colony with the aid of a Classicist poet and a Masonic lawyer. Like the other rulers of San Francisco, General Moncil is one-eyed. In search of monarchic stability, he wants to arrange a marriage of an arch-regal Iberian princess to a senile descendant of the Incas. There are historical bases for such a plan, but in *De milagros y de melancolías* it leads to the hero's loss of virginity and an unheroic assassination in a comedy of errors with sexual overtones.

From the era of civil strife, whose battles and murders are enumerated in imitation of the «begat» listing of the Bible, emerges a primitive Caudillo Bravaverga, who also had lost an eye. His supporters are long-haired Indians («jipis») and mestizo plainsmen («panchos»). He cows the patricians and the Church and marries two girls simultaneously. His regime also ends violently-dramatically, in fact in the theater.

The great Civilizer, a brilliant dwarf, loses his eye in a school hustle. He brings his country into the nineteenth century with absurd development schemes and a shaky railroad, but he is raped by his aunt and later marries a mute circus girl of his size. He too ends ignominiously after he joins his fifty-seven uncivilized half-brothers Vergas Bravas («Fearless Penises»), whom he is unable to subdue.

The last chapter is devoted to the vulgar demagogue, «El Líder», whose power bases are the football fans, the brothel operators, and the siesta-loving workers. Jealousy leads to his assassination, but not to the end of the book. The narrator's earlier interview with the one-eyed ruler included a spiritualist séance which forms the novel's Epilogue. In the latter we learn of the destruction of the city and its refounding in a timeless circle. There is also a celestial vision encompassing the past and future single-eyed heroes of the mythical San Francisco de Apricotina.

Even an outsider will notice echoes of Bolívar, Rosas, Sarmiento, and Perón in this resumé, but a Latin American will appreciate the comicality of demythologization in a host of details. Among them stands out the cult of mementos of the city's past. They are not only the relics connected with its questionable miracles but also grotesque civic ones. Existing heroic canvasses provided the inspiration for comical scenes, but Mujica Láinez obviously invented further tableaux, which are no less pictorial and humorous. The glories of America are deceptive, as we saw already in *Don Galaz*. The new novel makes it clear that humanity does not learn from history; passion for power, sensuality, and envy are the prime movers, with chance and error being major factors.

With this pessimistic outlook the writer produced in *De milagros* the funniest of all his works.[27] He put a certain distance between himself and sources, fake to be sure. This narrator —an exile and partisan of the murdered Líder, an opponent of «historical revisionism», and pompous local patriot— is himself highly unreliable. Mujica Láinez uses him to address with tongue-in-cheek, the saints-muses, the fatherland, the reader, and even the printer. This narrator is temporarily dramatized when he interviews the dictator at the latter's bordello-office. It is one of the

---

[27] Manuel Mujica Láinez, *De milagros y de melancolías* (Buenos Aires, 1968). This book will be cited by page number in the text and it may be referred to shortened to *De milagros*.

occasions when he uses the first person plural instead of the usual third-person account.

Within the general satirical tone one discerns a linguistic evolution, from an archaic, Cervantine Spanish, through Classicist rhetoric and Romantic passages to the popular speech of the time of the demagogue. The narrator's account is also quite self-conscious. He sees Fray Serafín as an allegory (18). He calls the liberating triumvirate a canvas (165). The doting Inca is a telluric metaphor (192) and the historic meeting with him is «staged» (196). The assassination of the Liberator is a parody of that of Danton (218). Finally, Doña Fidelidad is the «Deus ex machina» to put an end to the regime of the Caudillo (278).

Literature is not only imitated and parodied, as in the «Ode to the Liberator» (155 and passim) —memorized by the school children— and in the Neoclassic verses of a play, which helps to bring down the Bravaverga regime (267ff), it is borrowed liberally and literally from famous writers. These incongruous and anachronistic tidbits usually spice already comical circumstances. I find Borges (150), Silva (217), Darío (338), Neruda (410), and Manrique (416). Mujica Láinez not only parodies Magic Realism but he paraphrases one of its definitions, by Carpentier (293). This, to me, negates Wagman's thesis of an evolution to Magic Realism in the writer.

The humor of *De milagros* has been called Rabelaisian.[28] The book is full of grotesque situations, even grotesque deaths. Let us cite only an orgy interrupted by the playing of the national anthem, the midget Civilizer governing from a high chair, and the violent end of the Liberator and his family in the so-called «Gran Equivocación». Sex, too, is grotesque and it is more commonly heterosexual than otherwise. The culminating gag concerns the Duchess of Arpona who survived four hundred years on a diet of daily intercourse, but meets her doom in the City of Miracles. This, of course, brings us to the hints that time can be defeated, that it may not exist, or be circular, as suggested in the Epilogue.

Except in the cases of the long-lived Duchess and of the fantastic capability of the dwarf to produce reality by mere mental concentration —e.g. the instant erection of a protective Chinese Wall— magic and miracles receive perfectly natural explanations. Error looms large, as the gross pagan image comes to represent the Virgin, as native curing herbs turn out to be aphrodisiacs, or as the mature Princess and the old Inca consider marriage on the basis of portraits of their respective young representatives. Catalina's suicidal jump, after she learns her marriage to Baltasar would be incestuous, becomes a pious legend of angelic flight. Other familiar motifs, the drowning, the fire, the tapestry, reappear with a comical slant.

---

[28] Both by the writer himself and by VIRGINIA RAMOS FOSTER, in *Books Abroad*, 44 (1970), 82.

Even the immortality concept loses its sublimity when it is suggested the city's one-eyed leaders may only be one person reincarnated (232).

Captain Cintillo's sixteenth-century dreams of machines not yet invented amuse by their anachronism. Irony abounds, even in details: With historical scholarship being totally unreliable, it is uncertain how many colonial governors the city had; the number of their portraits is patently excessive. The Civilizer, wishing to spread progress evenly in the country, builds shipyards in the mountains and the College of Agriculture in the desert. The formation of the future Líder consists mainly of a homo- and heterosexual «safari» in Paris.

I could go on listing devices Mujica Láinez uses to demythologize South American history and society, but it must be noted that the almost excessive humor in *De milagros* is, to a great extent, one of language. The writer outdid his *Crónicas* in creating funny name: e.g. the daughters of the tax collector are named after revenues and Doña Fidelidad lacks fidelity. The book not only displays an extraordinary lexical richness, with archaisms, neologisms, double-entendres, contrasts, and incongruities, it even makes fun of lexical abundance and accuracy. The Royal Spanish Academy is cited for definitions; synonymic nouns, adjectives, and verbs are comically enumerated. Doña Salud's deathbed confession lists eighteen nouns other than beds denoting places for intercourse. Captain Cintillo drowns while looking for a suitable synonym for «boy», to be used in his chronicle.

From the foregoing it is clear that humor has become an end in itself in *De milagros y de melancolías*. The writer has used it quite heavy-handedly. The reader who can hardly stop laughing may laugh more about the form and language of the novel than about its content. One may wonder whether it really makes Latin Americans laugh heartily about themselves, which seems to have been the intent of Mujica Láinez. In an interview, between books, he referred to three critiques of reality, produced by great artists, the *Quijote, Gargantua,* and *Gulliver,* which represent «la fantasía al servicio de la crítica social».[29] *De milagros y de melancolías,* to a degree, became a political novel, but Villena rightly distinguishes it from Latin America's politicized literature by its cloak of irony and skeptic humor (24). Ghiano welcomed this return to critical humorism in Argentine letters.[30] Indeed, Latin Americans tend to take themselves and their literature too seriously. This may account, in part, for the only moderate success of Mujica Láinez's satire of 1969.

It also came at the wrong time. A year before the same publisher had launched *Cien años de soledad,* with which *De milagros y de melancolías*

---

[29] In *Confirmado,* 3 March 1971, with Pablo Aldazábal.
[30] «Mujica Láinez cronista de la América Meridional», *Sur,* 316-17 (1969), 99.

has much in common in scope and detail.[31] Mujica claims that he did not know the Colombian novel when he wrote his. García Márquez produced an international best seller, which eventually earned him the Nobel Prize. It was bound to eclipse the Argentine book which had less subtle irony and a highly complex satirical language.

As an outsider I would not be offended by Mujica Láinez's satire of the whole panoply of Spanish American traditions and I could enjoy it thoroughly. It does not represent the peak of universality in his production, but he could not possibly surpass the overflowing humor of *De milagros.* Henceforth he would dispense it in smaller, more efficient doses.

V. «EL LABERINTO»

The idea of concluding his anti-historical triptych with a book laid in the sixteenth century, in Spain or the America of the Conquest, must have been on the writer's mind for a long time. In interviews he alluded repeatedly to topics like Juana la Loca and to the Incas. But the project grew slowly and Mujica Láinez pursued other avenues before he wrote the third, quite different historical novel, in 1972. *El laberinto* won an international contest in Mexico, in 1973, but the novelist preferred to have it published in the same series as his other works. It came out in Buenos Aires in 1974.

In the interval after *De milagros y de melancolías* Mujica Láinez retired from *La Nación,* bought a villa in the interior of the country, and also moved his private collections to the mountains of Córdoba. This move and some health problems not only delayed the return to the trilogy but also augured a return to himself and more native themes. The time had not yet come for a full thematic homecoming, which will be discussed in the next chapter, but this return is already seen in the milieu and autobiographical nature of *Cecil,* which Mujica penned in 1971-72. Therefore, that book and a number of lesser items,[32] written at «El paraíso» in 1969-70, will not be analyzed in chronological sequence. Instead I will turn to the two books which still belong to the writer's universalist phase: the conclusion of the triptych, *El laberinto,* and the linked tales of *El viaje de los siete demonios,* both published in 1974.

In the midst of the composition of *El laberinto,* Mujica Láinez wrote to me, in English as he often did: «I want to construct (as I think I did in those two previous novels) a sound 'roman d'aventure'. My love

---

[31] See my article «The Four Hundred Years of Myths and Melancholies of Mujica Láinez», *Latin American Literary Review,* 1, No. 2 (1973), 65-71.

[32] The stories «Las alas», «El retrato», and «El brazalete», which were included in the *Brazalete* collection of 1978. Mujica Láinez also prologued an anthology of the writings of *Adolfo Mitre* and he published a translation of Racine's *Fedra.*

goes to books where things *happen* and *action* presides the whole conception».³³ In that respect the third panel of the triptych resembles the others, especially *El unicornio,* but there are marked differences. It is considerably shorter —approximately one hundred thousand words, which was becoming the writer's standard— and it is less complex. However, as a fresco of the Spanish Empire in the late sixteenth and early seventeenth centuries, it required copious documentation and its elaboration took eight and a half months.

The broad scope of *El laberinto,* which includes historical figures, places, and events, is camouflaged by its format. It is offered as the life story of Ginés de Silva, whose vicissitudes are related in the first person. His memoirs are merely «edited» by Mujica Láinez, who also appended a short note on the death of the protagonist. Don Ginés is born in Toledo in 1572 and dies in an historical battle near the novelist's country home in 1658. His long life span enables him to witness the splendors of an empire just past its prime, but his fortunes are mainly misfortunes, which he relates in a straightforward manner. He says his perspective is that of a typical Spaniard of the epoch,³⁴ whose quest for glory confronts him with the inglorious aspects of the age.

Ginés, therefore, is quite different from the immortality-seeking Duke and the immortality-burdened fairy of the other two historical novels, who even had a twentieth-century perspective. The modern tone is absent from *El laberinto.* Also don Ginés differs greatly from the neurotic don Galaz of the writer's first novel. The dramatized narrator of *El laberinto* is normal in every respect; he is a successful heterosexual and he seeks a fortune. Even the search for El Dorado has a very practical motive. One might say, too, within the overall frame of irony, his senile religious zeal seems perfectly normal for a man of his epoch. While the tone of that age is preserved, the language is not archaic, thanks to the editor. That editor is foreseen by the old soldier in his «Prologuete». This little prologue, which is headed by an epigraph from Juan de Mena's *Laberinto de fortuna,* sets the stage for a serio-comic autobiography, which views life as a labyrinth, with the eternal Minotaur of disenchantment lurking and with an inevitable outcome (10).

The novel's count of personages is high, as is usual with Mujica Láinez, but there is only one character, don Ginés, who superficially but effectively sketches everybody else. He himself slights his origins. His father is an impoverished hidalgo who craves honors and claims relatives of high nobility. He says his mother, an innkeeper's daughter, may have been the model for «La ilustre fregona» of Cervantes. Obviously, the life story

---

³³ In the letter cited in note 17 above.
³⁴ MANUEL MUJICA LÁINEZ, *El laberinto* (Buenos Aires, 1974), p. 216. This work also will be cited by page number in the text.

of this anti-hero has deep Hispanic roots. The latter are not only literary, as Ginés professes to have modelled for El Greco. He actually is the little boy with the torch in the lower left-hand corner of the famous «Entierro del Conde de Orgaz». His later masters are many and most varied, in the tradition of the Spanish rogue novel: a doltish grandee, whom he serves as a procurer; the great dramatist Lope de Vega, who uses him as valet and confidant; the Commander of the Invincible Armada, who makes him his page; and a pet shop owner, for whom he peddles exotic birds. Then, in America, he serves the new Viceroy of Peru; he works for a puppeteer in Quito and a slave trading ex-nun in Havanna; he participates in abortive expeditions; and he is obliged to marry a rich heiress in a forgotten outpost, Buenos Aires. Eventually, wishing to serve only God, he is forced to accompany an Indian insurrection to an ironic martyrdom on the wrong side.

The enumeration of these adventures already implies the structure of the book as a take-off of the picaresque novel. It is divided into eighteen main episodes in the life of the protagonist. The eighteen chapters form two equal parts, comprising the European and the American exploits. (Number eighteen pretends to be a third part, but it is merely the ninth American chapter, distinguished only by its fragmentary diary form and the memorialist's increasing senility.) The order is strictly chronological and there are no anachronisms — unless we consider the writing of such an historical novel in modern Buenos Aires itself an anachronism.

El laberinto, as another life under Philip II, also parodies *La gloria de don Ramiro,* of Larreta, under whose shadow the novelist had made his debut with *Don Galaz.*[35] Both Ramiro and Ginés start in Europe and die in the New World, but Mujica Láinez's book is evenly divided, while Larreta's ends with a last minute bow to America. Ramiro's glory is his repentant death, attended by Saint Rose of Lima, whereas Ginés dies a futile death in the wilderness. In spite of many parallels in motifs and technique, *El laberinto* clearly differs in its tone. Larreta's is a serious reconstruction of a great age of conflict, which even rages in the hero's mind; Mujica comically evokes the foibles of that age and his protagonist only struggles against adversity. Larreta's sincerity in his novel's pious ending may be questionable; Ginés's hope that his memoirs will serve as a lesson —«Aquí hallarás numerosos ejemplos de lo que no conviene a la salud del espíritu» near the end of the book (267)— is, of course, a standard picaresque conceit. His examples are largely sexual exploits and usually risible.

The comicality of Mujica Láinez's third triptych panel distinguishes it from the other two. It was clearly written after the satirical *Crónicas*

---

[35] Cf. «De la gloria de don Ramiro al desengaño de don Ginés», by GEORGE O. SCHANZER, in *Romance Literary Studies* (Potomac, MD, 1979), pp. 133-40.

and *De milagros*. However, instead of the boisterous humor of their linked episodes, especially in the language of the second, *El laberinto* manifests a pervasive irony, a sort of baroque patina of disenchantment. The author himself likes to call *Bomarzo* his most dramatic work, *Unicornio* the most poetic, and *El laberinto* the most ironic (*Mundo,* 108). This does not exclude grotesque elements. Here, to mention a few, belongs the case of the seasick commander of the «Felicísima Armada», who vomits over his page boy; here, too, is the chaperone who joins her charge and Ginés in bed and at the climax utters a shriek (a variant of Mujica's scream motif), followed by a night-time chase through Seville, with the naked Ginés, pretending to sleepwalk, pursued by guards. Likewise grotesque is the drowning of the narrator's vain wife, trapped in her hoopskirt.

In keeping with the picaresque tradition, most personages have common names, with two exceptions: Ginés' aunt is the widow of a Florentine adventurer, the Marquis Castracani («Dogspayer»), and the nickname of Manussio Theotocópuli, El Greco's brother, implies his homosexual designs, albeit unsuccessful in the case of Ginés.

Ginés also rejects Doña Bonitilla, who is really Don Bonitillo and, generally, advances from auto-erotism to a healthy heterosexuality. He differs from other protagonists of the writer in not being jeopardized by his great physical appeal. His multitude of partners are hardly individualized, not even the golden-hearted whore Micaela, who initiates him in the Cigarrales of Toledo. Ginés also has a chaste fixation on his dying father's young third wife, who soon after takes the veil. Her brother Gerineldo, perhaps a ballad-inspired character, becomes his life-long companion. The relationship seems somewhat ambiguous at start. Later Gerineldo, too, enjoys female company, but Ginés is not sufficiently privileged as a narrator to know whether his friend really has to sleep with their employer, the slave-trading ex-nun.

It must be already clear that the humor of *El laberinto,* open or subdued, lies mainly in people or things neither being what they appear or what they are supposed to be. This streak of irony, from the beginning to the end, is the hallmark of the book. We see it already when the Silva family leaves its rundown house to make a show of going to church: the ailing (syphilitic?) father, his widowed sister, the mannish duenna, and the (unpaid) squire. Even Toledo is no longer what it used to be when it was the capital of Spain. The writer attempts his usual guided tour and describes rituals and processions, but they do not convey the impression of grandeur.

In Madrid, Ginés sees the splendor of the Royal Palace only in its dwarfs and buffoons. The Wandering Jew appears again, but in the last book of the trilogy this constant of Mujica Láinez is a vulgar impostor. The model for King Philip's portrait, by El Greco, is a madman from the asylum. But Ginés himself sells a copy of a Greco painting as an authentic Greco, in a pinch.

Bonitillo/Bonitilla —perhaps a parody of the «mujer vestida de hombre» of Golden Age literature— is patently unauthentic, but inspires Lope de Vega to compose the authentic *La hermosura de Angélica*. Even the pursuit of El Dorado is parodied in *El laberinto*. Only Ginés, a survivor of the expedition, has a hallucinatory vision of the golden-skinned cacique, with sexual overtones to boot. In the end, the leader of the Indian rebellion is a false Inca, an historical impostor — who inveigles the would-be missionaries Ginés and Gerineldo.

The great Armada is incredibly mismanaged; the recruitment for the El Dorado expedition is fraudulent. The vastness of America is real but its treasures are a hoax. Religion too is suspect. Saint Teresa of Avila's miraculous transfixion is repeated by Ginés' aunt; her garments become commercialized relics; and she dies in the odor of sanctitiy. Finally, her incredulous nephew, too, believes in her miracles. The Wandering Jew uses an Indian mummy to exploit live natives, who, although trained to fake adoration, then adore the embalmed. The most satirical treatment of religion, specifically the rite of Extreme Unction as practised in Hispanic lands to «ayudar a bien morir», is seen in Chapter V, when Ginés, with a lantern, escorts a prostitute across Madrid to «ayudar a bien dormir» the insomniac grandee, his employer.

Devices familiar from previous works of the writer re-emerge in *El laberinto* in a hilarious context. The «I was there» technique, serious in the Lepanto scenes of *Bomarzo,* is tragicomic in those of the defeat of the Invincible Armada. There are other encounters: with an historical pirate, with Garcilaso de la Vega, with the future Saint Martín de Porres, and with the poet Luis de Tejeda. In connection with Ginés' serving as janitor in Madrid's Corral de Comedias and his involvement in Lope's private scandals, we even find quotations from a play. Considering the distances and the time elapsed, re-encounters are amazing: the transvestite, the Wandering Jew, and Baltasar reappear two or three times. The inclusion of an incredibly fat woman will not surprise, but the lithe Gerineldo, too, ends up impeded by obesity.

On the whole *El laberinto* manifests a pessimistic view, which is cheerfully expounded in a traditional form and style. Discounting his youthful imitations of Azorín, in the *Glosas,* and of Larreta, in *Don Galaz,* the third panel of his anti-historical triptych is Mujica Láinez's most Hispanic work. It affords a somewhat irreverent but most pleasurable reading, especially for a public familiar with its heritage.

El laberinto has been reprinted several times. It was very well received by the critics at home and abroad. Fellow novelist Silvina Bullrich called it one of the writer's most felicitously accomplished works.[36] An American scholar of Argentine literature noted its undeniable novelistic mastery.[37] The book is beyond the scope of the studies by Font and Wagman. The latter could not have found any Magic Realism in its historical vision. It is surprising, however, that none of the commentators of *El laberinto* stressed its picaresque affiliation, as I did in a review[38] and here. It is, after *La casa,* the most satisfactory of Mujica Láinez's novels and the most balanced of his works of the universalist phase.

VI. «EL VIAJE DE LOS SIETE DEMONIOS»

The scope of Mujica Láinez's next book could hardly be more universal. It encompasses the whole globe geographically, its historic time ranges from 79 A.D. to the twenty-third century. Even a tireless world traveller and history buff like Mujica had to prepare it carefully. According to Cruz (160) it took much of 1973 to write it, although it is shorter than *El laberinto.* Both were published in 1974.

El viaje de los siete demonios opens and closes in hell. The writer knew the other locations, including Siberia, from journalistic assignments. There is a pretense that we are dealing with a travel book —the devils themselves are looking forward to more «turismo pecador»[39]— but the book's cover, taken from a medieval canvas, makes it clear that it is some sort of allegory or modern take-off of the morality tales of old.

Mujica Láinez denies any didactic intent by using an epigraph from Juan Valera, which makes the reader responsible for any moral he would draw from a book meant to entertain, not to teach. But *El viaje* is not a novel; nor is it a mere collection of allegorical tales. Foster called its structure «archaic, medieval», yet appropriate for the writer's «mordant, sardonic, and almost misanthropic vision of mankind».[40] The highly structured work is composed of a Prologue and seven sections —each labelled «Viaje»— which alternate with seven longer accounts of seduction. The latter bear the names of the devils and the sins in which they specialize. However, the seven devils travel jointly and act as a team. The somewhat shorter travel sections are not mere links but essential to the overall topic of a recruitment tour, ordered by their chief, the Devil with capital «D». Therefore, in *El viaje* we find action —the seductions— alternating

---

[36] «El color de una época», *La Nación*, 7 July 1974.
[37] DAVID WILLIAM FOSTER, *Books Abroad,* 49 (1975), 516.
[38] *Latin American Literary Review,* 4, No. 7 (1975), 92-94.
[39] MANUEL MUJICA LÁINEZ, *El viaje de los siete demonios* (Buenos Aires, 1974), p. 298. Further quotations will be cited by page number in the text.
[40] DAVID WILLIAM FOSTER, *Books Abroad,* 49 (1975), 524.

with comment, sometimes highly whimsical, ideological observations, in a structure much tighter than that of autonomous linked tales.

For a change, Mujica Láinez composed a book written in the third person without a separate narrator. Also, there is no central protagonist, only seven pairs of tempters and victims. The former are the timeless devils; the latter are very much anchored in time and place. The stops on the journey are not pre-arranged but randomly determined by a drawing of the sin to be induced next, by a timeclock, and by a map.

The first stop is in Poitou, in 1443, where Lucifer (in charge of Pride) makes the widow of the pervert and wholesale murderer Gilles de Rais pursue his canonization. Then Mammon (Greed) causes the destruction of Pompeii, in 79 A.D., in which the denizens lose their lives trying to save their treasures. Next is Leviathan (Envy), who makes the Dowager Empress of China, in 1898, destroy the power of her successor, out of resentment. Belcebú (Gluttony) debauches an ascetic hermit in Bolivia's Potosí, in 1865, with a fantastic banquet. Satan (Ire) releases the pent-up anger of a Venetian majordomo against his master, in 1764. A most punctilious French official is aroused by Asmodeus (Lust) in the West Indies, in 1647. Finally, Belfegor, the diabolic personification of Sloth, brings the whole globe to a halt in the Siberia of 2273. In this festive allegory the rotation of the earth is re-started by a joint effort of angels and devils, to assure the supply of souls. The Devil, taking no chances, suspends further tours of his subordinates, ironically invoking God.

From the foregoing it is obvious that Mujica Láinez again played with time, which the Devil calls «una absurda convención de los hombres» (27). This also opens the door for the use of many delightful anachronisms, of foreknowledge, and of a contemporary perspective. However, pre-Christian seductions are absent, since the book is structured on the classification of sins, according to Christian theology — which the writer, no doubt with a smile, assumes as a premise. But he has the hellish executive (in his grey-flannel suit, in an excessively air-conditioned office) wonder whether the confidential information on the seven devils and the respective sins may have been «leaked» to the theologians. The concern of the devils about the possible penances of their victims implies, ironically, another Catholic tenet.

Only when it comes to the devil's means of transportation does the writer go beyond Christianity to dip into ancient myths. The travellers' mounts include a griffin, an Assyrian bull, and a mermaid, plus a team of apes. These transporters also afford the book's best political satire when they form a labor union, elect a shop steward (the mermaid), and achieve nothing. The apes conveying Belfegor —Laziness of undetermined sex but predominantly female— take an unauthorized vacation, but Belfegor continues, floated from New York's Empire State tower by means on inflated, multi-colored condoms.

The process of debasing sex in Mujica Láinez's works has reached its culmination in *El viaje*. It is not merely one in a catalogue of heinous sins. It is even used as a punishment: Dante's famous adulterous lovers Paolo and Francesca are forced by their hellish tormentors to copulate three times daily. Other remarks make sex appear ambiguous, humiliating, even sadistic. Lust provoked by Asmodeo, in Section XII, is a most solitary one. One might say, sensuality is one of the human weaknesses that does not appear funny in this entertaining volume.

In general, the book's comicality lies not so much in the victims' (predictable) fall but in the «superhuman» efforts of the devils to tempt them. In the case of Lust, Asmodeo puts on a great «show» [sic]. This affords an opportunity for an outpouring of lascivious conjurations of all times and places, preceded by a repast of aphrodisiacs and supported by other media, such as music and fragrance. With the writer's penchant for enumeration, cumulative or chaotic, this becomes a virtuoso performance. It exceeds even the lavish gastronomic cataloguing of the Gluttony section.

Mujica Láinez also indulged in his love for the dramatic in *El viaje*. The devils improvise constantly; they disguise instantly; they put on pantomimes and even dreams in the sleep of their recalcitrant targets. They assume supporting roles, e.g. «sustituyendo..., pero no anulando...; conservando las trazas» (135) of Chinese princesses in a phenomenon suggestive of the transubstantiation of the Catholic faith. One episode, the explosion of anger in Section X, hinges on the performance of an entire Commedia dell'Arte in a Venetian palace. This enables Sior Leonardo, the illegitimate son of several possible most noble fathers, to improvise the downgrading of his employer, a man of rather recent nobility. It is a play within a play within an allegorical narrative.

The Venetian section, naturally, alludes to Goldoni, one of the numerous literary hints, take-offs, quotes, and parodies in the book. Given the subject, it will not surprise that the devils belittle Dante and Milton; that they check the accuracy of Lytton in Pompeii and of Stevenson on the treasure island; that Ortega is used for antidemocratic remarks and that Borges is transparent in allusions to endless, facing mirrors and to dreams within dreams. Reality, as seen or created by the writer, is to check the preciseness or authenticity of a text or a work of art. Here belong the cases of the superiority of Mujica Láinez's version of the suffering of the senile adulterers in hell, of the ecology of Tortuga Island, and of the Pompeian statue of the Faun — supposedly the work of one devil and representing another.

Judging from his publisher's statistics, Mujica Láinez seems to have a faithful audience. Therefore, his readers will enjoy finding in *El viaje* allusions to Melusina, a castle fit for a vampire, a hunchback, a one-eyed personage, an ignorant caudillo, etc. They will note the numerous pictorial scenes and wonder, at times, whether the writer describes a Bosch, Breughel, or Dalí canvas or whether he is inventing new ones. The devils themselves are aware that they represent existing allegorical engravings or that their poses should be preserved for eternity in the works of artists. The book also shows the usual Modernist concern with the chromatic, with sheen, and with ceremonies. The latter, of course, are diabolically hieratic and, like everything else, comical. So is Mujica's resumé when the devils show the chief the album of photos taken on their tour. (A few are missing and will become the subject of subsidized research in the United States!)

The treatment of machines in *El viaje* is more than comical. It manifests Mujica Láinez's profound suspicion of things technical. Hell, viewed from aloft, seems a heavy industrial plant and the world of the future —Siberia in 2273— shows that human wisdom can attain a perfect reproduction of the social paradigm of Hell.

While *El viaje* is not a book with a message, its entertaining pages contain much of the writer's philosophy: there are no perfect creatures; passions won't change; even the most steadfast humans succumb to temptation; devils can make mistakes and angels can be careless.

Much of this comment appears in the «Viaje» sections, which are full of witticism and clever repartee, and are also the author's preference (*Mundo,* 116). Never before has Mujica Láinez written that much and that good dialogue, as the touring devils constantly tease each other and each claims the superiority of his sin. When they take a stand, idiosyncratically, parallelistic structures ensue, which are highly comical. But the most significant ideas are expressed by individual devils: Belfegor insists «en el derecho a la pereza reside el derecho a la libertad» (294); Lucifer asserts «el hombre es una creación de Dios, retocado por el Diablo» (203). This seems also the basic idea which permeated the entire work. There is a need for both; Heaven and Hell are competitors, not enemies; they have to cooperate to restore the rotation of the earth. The dualism of Mujica Láinez's humorous allegory brings to mind «El reino interior» of Rubén Darío, where the soul wishes to embrace both the cardinal sins and the cardinal virtues.[41]

On the whole, *El viaje de los siete demonios* is an «Infernal Comedy» of human foibles. It makes light of everything, from ancient myths to modern politics, from Prometheus to Mao. Among all the sophisticated

---

[41] The author told MARÍA ESTHER VÁZQUEZ that he hoped to conclude «El escarabajo» «con la ayuda de los ángeles y demonios necesarios». When she asked him «¿Tenés muchos ángeles y muchos demonios?» he replied [*sic*]: «Half and half» (*Mundo,* 187).

frivolity there is profound irony: the seven princes of the nether world, who address each other as «Comrade Excellence», have to work hard to achieve their ends. (The Pompeian section, which required the least effort, is saved by the fantasy of clever detail. It was Villena's choice for inclusion in his anthology. Mine would be No. X, the Venetian chapter.)

I do not know how the book fared after its first printing was sold out. Critical reaction has been uneven. The Quevedo-like humor reigning in the volume was noted by only one Argentine critic.[42] Indeed, the humor of *El viaje de los siete demonios* is more one of conceits than situational or lexical. In spite of its appeal to sophisticated readers, I have to agree with Foster who felt, in his review cited above, that Mujica Láinez had pretty well exhausted «the possibilities of the curious vignettes-on-human-frailties-and-debaucheries modes of fiction». The writer himself may have felt that way and he turned to other avenues.

---

[42] ALBA OMIL, «El pensamiento mágico y su mitología», *La Gaceta,* undated clipping, found in the library of the Argentine Academy.

5

COMING HOME

As I have noted before, Mujica Láinez reordered his life in the pause between *De milagros* and his next book. He acquired a neglected estate on a hillside in a resort area at a night ride's distance from Buenos Aires —just close enough to and far enough from the attractions and the demands of the metropolis. His relation with *La Nación* changed to that of a freelance contributor's, mainly of travelogues.

The move to «El Paraíso», as the villa happened to be called, without any connection to the fourth of the Saga novels, was the great project of 1969-1971. It was also a time of returning to himself, to his family, and to his roots. On the estate he was accompanied by his wife and his aged mother, his three aunts, and he was surrounded by mementos of family and national history, largely intertwined, as well as by art objects from all over the world. He also installed his library of 20,000 books and ordered his files and albums. «El Paraíso» became a veritable museum and a monument to himself. Perhaps he wished to surpass the fictional collectors he had created with his own, priceless, tasteful, and quite personal holdings which fill the villa from top to bottom. Yet the displacement and taking stock wearied the writer and he could not decide for some time on a topic for another book. He had not retired to withdraw; indeed, he entertained friends and even reporters, but he was wistful, roaming the hills with his dog Cecil.

I. «CECIL»

Cecil is a reflection of this uneasiness and it is also a description of the writer at home and at work as seen by his dog. Cecil, the real Cecil, whose picture is on the cover, is the narrator of the book. The topic is his master, «el Escritor» (capitalized), the Squire of «El Paraíso». The time is that of the composition, more or less.

The book was written in three and a half months in late 1971 and early 1972. Four months later the slight volume —about fifty thousand words— was in print. It is a book difficult to classify. Its nineteen divisions range from two to thirty-nine pages in size and are mainly episodic or descriptive, as is much of Mujica Láinez's work. But they also include the biography of a decadent Roman emperor and the retelling of an ancient Greek myth. What holds *Cecil* together is the dog's observing the creative process. He does quite a bit of musing about his own existence, but it is not Cecil's autobiography. Nor is it an autobiography of the writer who invents a first-person canine narrator to present the text. The publisher refrained from calling it a novel but quoted Mujica who called it an «autobiografía novelesca».[1] I prefer to call it a fictionalized self-portrait, because a real autobiography was never written. (The first section of his 1967 record[2] bears that label, but it was very limited.) In *Cecil* we see the writer at sixty, trying to produce another book. Villena may have hit the mark by considering it «a novel about a novel» (29), something not uncommon in contemporary literature.

Cecil is the most personal of the novelist's works. It is by design fiction but at the same time replete with real people, objects, and happenings. It faithfully relates, as seen by the dog, Manucho's and Anita's establishing themselves in the mountains of Córdoba. This includes truckers bringing an unusual statue, the antics of an adopted, stray, one-eyed (!) cat, and the visit of a grantee of an American university with a doctoral project on Mujica Láinez's irony (which, ironically, was never finished).

The book also tells, without apparent effort to fictionalize them, of curious people that inhabit, year-round, the resort area, a lot as cosmopolitan as Buenos Aires, mainly British, French, and German retirees. Their native language phrases and idiosyncrasies abound in the text, and the Writer, according to Cecil, converses with them about a variety of cultural topics. «El Paraíso» also came with a ghost, whose presence is strongly felt by the dog. «El fantasma de Mr. Littlemore» is the ghost of an Englishman, whose wife had served him poisoned tea. There is also an evocation of a previous owner of the estate, a very obese lady, who is imagined as a ripe odalisk bathing in the now-neglected pool. With the numerous real personages (relatives, friends, neighbors, visitors, and pets) intermingle the supernatural ones and the imaginary protagonists of the writer's projects which are eventually aborted.

The most interesting feature of this book between books is Cecil's capability of seeing potential literary characters. He is, to be sure, a very unusual narrator, although Mujica Láinez's earlier ones, the House, the re-incarnated Duke, and the Fairy, were not exactly conventional either.

---

[1] On the back cover of *Cecil* (Buenos Aires, 1972), likewise to be cited in the text by page number.
[2] «Manuel Mujica Láinez por él mismo», AMB Discográfica, 1967.

Now, the anthropomorphic treatment of animals, even their discussing humans, is as old as literature itself and it is also seen in the book's epigraph, taken from Cervantes' «Coloquio de los perros». But Cecil is a special dog. He is a whippet, a small English greyhound of an ancient lineage, going back to the Egypt of old. He has a lot in common with his master: the slight build, the pedigree, the concern with things British, with oriental symbols, and with Modernist decorative backgrounds. He is a bit of a snob and, like Pier Francesco, an alter ego of the writer. However, he is the first to picture him at work and to compete with other creations of his mind. It is a sort of doubling process, in which the double not only has a dog's loyalty but a passionate attachment, so much so that Cruz rightly refers to «narcisismo» in his review of the book.[3] The whippet is also jealous of real humans, especially of Mujica's young male friends, but he joyously accepts the imaginary beings which are the products of his master's mind. (He has a mild disdain for Anita's mongrel bitch.)

Whereas the general reader will enjoy the observations of the canine narrator and the refined prose and irony of Mujica Láinez, the critic will be intrigued by his insight into the working of «the Writer's» creative mind. It is a dog's perspective on the writing of a novel; rather, how his master writes a novel. It will not surprise us that Cecil's insight is entirely visual. He himself says: «me sitúo... en el cinematógrafo de su cabeza» (20). The imaginative fragments of the stories or novels to be written or to be discarded —for *Cecil* is also the dumping ground for literary fetuses not carried to term— are movie scenes rather than glimpses of character or plot. They are pictorial and dramatic; some have the makings of a multi-million-dollar movie. When the master is away, the «performances» cease and the dog is lonely. (I saw Cecil in the writer's absence and he seemed a shy, insignificant animal.) Periods of Mujica's reduced activity depress the devoted narrator; he is elated when his master very actively projects images.

The images may be merely superimposed on present reality. In that case the dog sees people and circumstances at «El Paraíso» modified in his master's imagination, i.e. they become potential fictional characters and situations. The gestation is more advanced when a story is «retold», of course in the writer's best ironic prose, such as «Aquiles en la Isla de las Mujeres» (Chapter XV). It is inspired by the arrival at the villa of a statue of the mythical Greek hero. That copy of the French original sculpture of 1695 shows the adolescent Achilles dressed as a girl. Cecil refers to Mujica's limited inquiries about the topic and then states «Esta es la historia» (161), which introduces its re-elaboration. Briefly: in

---

[3] JORGE CRUZ, in *La Nación*, 13 August 1972.

order to avoid Achilles being drafted for the Trojan War, his mother disguises him as a maiden and hides him on an island among the daughters of its king. He impregnates one of them, but, after being discovered by tricky Ulysses, goes off to war.

The creative process is much more complex in the case of another transvestite, the «Historia del Emperador Heliogábalo» (Chapter XVI). It makes up one-sixth of the entire book, is set apart completely in italics, and is also preceded by an account of the extensive research and documentation which went into its elaboration. (This is not a fictitious bibliography, as seen in *De milagros,* but a listing of twenty-two serious works, old and new —several in English— including a collection of papers by American historians.) The material enabled the writer to compose a biography of the ill-famed emperor, which the dog states, «mi amo destinó a ser utilizada como guía cuando entrase de lleno en el trabajo de su ficción» (119). In other words, the chapter is just the framework of a novel that was never written.

Another topic never seems to have progressed farther than to a couple of movie-like scenes from the life of the Mad Queen, «Dos visitas de la Reina Juana» (Chapter XVIII), with «un entreacto corto» (201) between them and projection discontinued because of the master's weariness. These images —the surrender of Granada and the wedding preparations in Burgos, where the petitioning Columbus is ignored— had been stimulated by a record of Spanish Renaissance music.

In the foregoing examples the glimpses of the creative process showed at least some of its results. But in this intensely self-conscious narrative there are sections in which there are none. They deal with the process itself and with its vicissitudes. «Fracasos del Escritor» (V) picture his anxieties, the hard times between books, and the fear that the last work may be the last. Many of these are not perceived intuitively by the dog but appear as a five-page statement, enclosed by quotation marks, probably made to visiting journalists and also published in some journal or other. (There is no indication of what came first, the interview or the book.) In the same chapter Mujica also remarks that it was *Crónicas reales* which opened for him «la puerta de un mundo... de la ironía pura, el de la sátira» (48). He also hints at books in the making, a topic spilling over into «Espectros de la Literatura» (VI). There Cecil observes his master's struggling to have his images come to literary life. One cannot help remembering the strenuous effort of the Civilizer, in *De milagros,* who erects a Chinese Wall by mental concentration, but is too weary to maintain it.

In a work concerned primarily with the problem of literary creation, the absence of a clear plot and structure is not surprising. There is a book to be written, but the text we are reading could vary. There could be additions, subtractions, substitutions, even transpositions; what is essential, however, is its circularity. The book being gestated is the book we have read. *Cecil* ends with the same paragraph with which it began. The whippet is elated when he looks over his master's shoulder and sees him writing the first lines of his own story. By a neat trick the muse has become the subject and narrator and author are one, as at the close of *Bomarzo*.

The triumphant entry of Heliogabalus in Rome brings to mind the coronation scene of that Renaissance novel, but the teenage emperor is infinitely more dazzling and perverted than the Duke. Mujica Láinez's choice of another bisexual protagonist with a homosexual preference, in a setting of splendorous decadence, seems deliberate. It is interesting to note that, in one of the key works of Spanish American Modernism, Rubén Darío expressed an interest in the decadent Roman emperor (*Prosas profanas,* «Palabras preliminares»). There is a suggestion of ambiguity also in the Achilles tale and elsewhere.

The constant of mysticism is seen in the Syrian ruler's role as a high priest, which facilitates likewise the Modernist stress on nudity, rituals, and processions. The motif of tourism appears in the excursions taken by the master-dog pair. There is even a guided visit — this time not as a final summary but as a presentation of the treasures of «El Paraíso» (IV). The guide's «spiel» is always the same, notes the dog. We find links to other works of the writer, both past and future, and many clever statements, such as the one which calls legend «auxiliar poética de la Historia» (71). Mujica Láinez himself is aware that he is becoming a legend and both he and the dog are conscious of a certain theatrality.

Cecil amuses but it is a far cry from the grotesque humor of the preceding *De milagros*. Its constant irony, especially in the inserts (Heliogabalus, Achilles) is closer to that of the following *Laberinto*. As in the cases of Mujica Láinez's other works of the 1970s, criticism is still rather limited. Some local reviewers called the author of *Cecil* an esoteric medieval writer in the twentieth century, and, with their political stance, deplored his reactionary, escapist attitude.[4] But the book impressed an American expert in the Latin American narrative[5] and Villena saw in it the keys to Mujica Láinez's universe. He suggested that *Cecil* should be the last book in a complete reading of all the works of the writer (29-31). Of course, at the time *El viaje* was the last. Perhaps in line with Villena's thinking, I consider *Cecil* more a book for the critic than for the ordinary reader.

---

[4] Among others, HORACIO SALAS, «Un hombre enamorado de sí mismo», *Clarín*, 7 September 1973.

[5] KESSEL SCHWARTZ, *Hispania*, 57 (1974), 186. Schwartz compares Mujica's fusing the abstract with the real to the techniques of García Márquez and Cortázar.

II. «SERGIO»

The novel *Sergio* appealed to a broad audience and soon became a sort of best-seller. Written after *El laberinto* and *El viaje* —as well as after another trip of Mujica Láinez to the lands East of Venice— the new work completed the writer's homecoming. It is Argentine to the core, composed in the Sierra de Córdoba and opening there, with a protagonist who hails from the interior, who roams the world, and who meets a tragic fate in Buenos Aires. There is also a change of fictional time. In an interview cited by Cruz (165), the novelist himself stated: «He salido de mis acostumbrados temas históricos para zambullirme en lo contemporáneo.» *Sergio* is not only his most contemporary work, it is also somewhat partisan politically; moreover, it is the most openly homosexual one in his long creative career, according to Mujica's admission (*Mundo,* 118).

The writer spent the first half of 1976 on this novel, which had its first, rather large printing later that year. The compact volume, slightly larger than *Cecil,* is well structured with ten chapters of fairly even size and an epilogue. The ten divisions correspond to episodes in the short life of the youth, Sergio. The topic, supposedly, was inspired in a dream, which Mujica Láinez jotted down on awakening. This became the outline of the novel, according to the conversation cited above. Its characters and scenes, more than ever, blend the writer's own reality with fiction. It must have made the readers wonder which figures of Buenos Aires and the world may have become secondary personages in the book to surround the fictional Sergio. In the fragmentized society of the post-Perón era, this constituted a further attraction.

The Argentina of the 1970s is only the satirized setting of *Sergio.* Its theme was correctly identified in the title of one of its reviews as «Las tribulaciones de la hermosura».[6] This, of course, recalls the trials of Aiol, of *El unicornio,* and the novelist's perennial concern with handsome youths. In the case of Sergio, his unusual attractiveness is rather a curse.

Sergio is a conventional book with few unconventional features. It has a third-person narrator who is omniscient enough to fathom the psychology of the protagonist, to a great extent also that of his companion, Juan, and, to a much lesser degree, the latter's sister Soledad. This narrator also shows great sympathy for these adolescents; he seems to scorn the minor characters with all their human foibles. Mujica Láinez is very much present in his book, through the probing, pitying, and chuckling narrator and even as a secondary personage. He is alluded to as the «escritor medio loco»[7] who ordered a bust from the antique dealer

---

[6] Delfín Leocadio Garassa, *La Nación,* 9 January 1977.
[7] Manuel Mujica Láinez, *Sergio* (Buenos Aires, 1976), p. 133. Further quotations in the text itself.

— the statue which graces the approach to the villa in *Cecil*. Also, unnamed, he appears in person at a party, in the writer's familiar finery (black velvet coat and monocle). Finally, accompanied by a friend known from *Cecil*, he accidentally meets Sergio and Juan in the Prado Museum of Madrid, with an important message from home. Again, Mujica Láinez included himself in his fiction.

The novelistic time of *Sergio* spans the years between the youth's emergence at fourteen and his untimely death, at twenty-two, as a bystander during a shoot-out in the turbulent days prior to the military take-over of 1976. This makes the outcome of the book coincide, more or less, with the start of its composition. Never before had Mujica Láinez been so greatly concerned with his compatriots' daily preoccupations. Sergio may be a dreamer, but he and Juan have to think about military service and permission to go abroad. Whereas Juan sympathizes with his leftist colleagues at the university, Sergio hopes for a «dictadura honesta» (153). Near the end, they hear from «the writer» about murders, kidnappings, blackmail and corruption back home, but also about the hope that law and order would soon be restored by the military (232). It is ironic (and typical of Mujica Láinez) that Sergio does not live to see this and that he falls victim, erroneously, of an old acquaintance, a ministerial bodyguard. This is quite in line with the novelist's concept of destiny as a dramatic producer and of error as a decisive force. Besides, from my own impressions of Argentina in 1976, an accidental death then, in cross fire, does not appear overly melodramatic but entirely plausible.

Spatially, the action of *Sergio* takes place in the country, in the city, and in significant foreign locations. The constant shifts of scene not only reflect Mujica Láinez's own lifestyle but also echo, for the first time, the deeply rooted antagonism between the Argentine capital and the hinterland (as well as between provinces). For the friars of Córdoba, who offer refuge to Sergio, the metropolis is «la gran hembra apocalíptica lujuriosa» (57). We also get a glimpse of the Argentines abroad, but the only places described in loving detail (Venice and Ravenna) had been the topics of the writer's recent travelogues. There is no attempt to describe landscapes, but, in the Modernist fashion, much attention is given to sumptuous interiors, such as the Moreno residence —another *Casa*— the scene of the «Cocktail-party» [*sic*] (V) and the antique shop. Other world cities, Sidney, Vienna, Monaco, and the homes of the jet set —Mrs. Onassis, the Shah, etc.— are mentioned only in passing. Yet there is a curious tie-in between fiction and reality, when the traveller stops in Paris at the home of Leonor Fini, who happens to have provided the cover design for the book.

From the foregoing it would seem that Sergio is a hero always on the go. However, the truth is the opposite; he is no hero and his moves are consecutive escapes. The major episodes in his errant life make up the plot of the novel. A beautiful, blue-eyed mestizo «de una provincia remota, donde la Argentina se volvía indiscutiblemente latinoamericana» (39), Sergio is the target of relentless pursuits of major and minor characters. The term persecution, used by one critic,[8] is not appropriate, since his successive sponsors do not seek to destroy him but to incorporate him into their lives and life styles. Also, Sergio does not aim to live at their expense; therefore, the same reviewer also erred in calling his wanderings picaresque. However, the largely sexual exploitation of the youth by a gallery of representative types does make the book, to a degree, «una novela de costumbres contemporáneas».[9] Still, Sergio's curse is not only beauty; he is unable to make decisions and he tends to walk in his sleep. The strange introversion does not prevent the bright orphan from Catamarca from becoming accomplished in music, Latin, French, and social graces. It increases the erotic fascination he unwittingly causes around him.

He is first discovered as an ephebic somnambulist on the cornice of a resort hotel. An elderly British minister and a mature Jewish piano teacher vie for rescuing the pubescent country boy. The lusty European refugee wins and takes Sergio to Buenos Aires. There she manages to possess him in a drugged state. Since she has been the mistress of an aging German Nazi baron (who hides the Führer's picture from her as she conceals the menorah from him) obvious complications arise. In a scene reminiscent of one in *El laberinto,* the unclad, awakening Sergio flees from the ardent pianist into the night. He is saved by a jolly, visiting friar, who takes him to his seminary in Córdoba. He expects the youth to become a saintly classical scholar and, in a couple of years, Sergio does acquire both polish and some classical culture. However, masturbation causes such guilt feelings in him that he runs away. At the resort, where his aunt works, the sensitive youth feels ill at ease. He reencounters the secret service man Guadagni, whom he met at the baron's house, and develops a chaste infatuation for Guadagni's new bride. When the Reverend Light asks him to go with him to spread the Gospel, he follows the British minister to Buenos Aires, but, after repelling his homosexual advances, he again finds himself alone in the big city.

He is taken in by a former fellow student of the piano, who had become a playboy. This catapults Sergio into high society. José Luis' mother is preparing a reception to honor a visiting celebrity. The son is preparing a minor orgy with two little whores and, under the influence of liquor, Sergio definitely loses his virginity. He is also pursued by his

---

[8] ALDRICH MACADAM, *Handbook of Latin American Studies,* 40 (1978), 425.
[9] See note 6 above.

friend's spinster cousin. The visiting philosopher, perhaps modelled after Ortega y Gasset, becomes another great disappointment for Sergio, whose life is a series of seductions and disillusions. Yet in this world of rich ladies, who play arbiters of culture —a world Mujica Láinez knows best— Sergio meets an antique dealer who offers him a job.

In the refined setting of the shop, the youth gets to know the owner's teenage children, Juan and Soledad. Sergio is attracted to both and they to him. In this strange three-way attachment —an «artifice» repeatedly used by the author (*Mundo*, 119)— Sergio is confused and passive and Juan the driving force. When the father fires Sergio, suspecting him of corrupting Juan, the latter makes Sergio flee to the mountains with him. The two find peace neither with the friars nor at the resort and join a group of itinerant players. However, an actor lusts for Sergio and a married actress for Juan and the friends make another escape to return to the city. They find the antiquarian conciliatory, as Soledad is about to marry the playboy — on the rebound, it seems, since Sergio and Juan had abandoned her.

At the wedding reception Sergio meets «the writer» and the renowned pianist Rothenstein (Rubinstein?). Afterwards the erotic relationship of Juan and Sergio is finally consummated, perhaps also on the rebound. The protagonist awakens with the realization «Hemos cometido un gran pecado» (187). Sergio again avoids commitment by accepting Rothenstein's offer to accompany him. He does not know yet that the virtuoso, too, uses him to attract women in his travels all over the world. This has erotic fringe benefits for the secretary, but Sergio remains aloof, dreaming of Juan and Soledad.

Juan catches up with him in Venice to tell him of the antiquarian's death. So Sergio runs away from the pianist's last wild party to return to Buenos Aires. On the way home, the pair are invited by an eccentric British lady to attend a spiritist séance in Ravenna. At that session (which brings to mind the Modernists' fascination with the topic) Sergio is promised an important encounter and cautioned against something sounding like the «scythe of death» («guadaña»). Naturally, the friends encounter «the writer» in Madrid, with the news of Soledad's divorce. Sergio's hope for a *ménage à trois* is cut short when, on return to Argentina, the friends are gunned down, in error, by Aniceto Guadagni.

In his «contemporary» novel Mujica Láinez has spun an interesting yarn of basically linear progression, with a few fill-ins of background information. He used what could be called a nineteenth-century technique of surprises, coincidences, and re-encounters. But with it he satirically sketched a multitude of settings: the worlds of Jewish and Nazi refugees, naive monks, hypocritical puritans, playboys and female culture czars, the primitive creole theater, the antique business, and the international lecture and concert circuits. In spite of the fulfillment of the predictions, neither the spiritists nor the bodyguard escape the novelist's satire. The prediction itself is based on a pun. Nevertheless, Sergio is a pessimistic rather than a humorous book. There are dramatic confrontations and some grotesque scenes: e.g. the baron unpacks his Nazi uniform, after expelling his Jewish lover, and salutes the Führer's picture. We also find the merging of art and reality, seen in earlier works, when Sergio projects himself into the famous Velázquez painting «Las Meninas» in the Prado Museum. Still, none of these details can explain the great success of the novel, which has not yet had more than routine reviews.

I see in it more than a novel of adolescent sexual confusion. Its deeper significance may be more apparent at a distance. To me, Sergio — the mestizo from inland, handsome, bright, dreamy, adrift in the cosmopolitan city, in a world obsessed with sex; the insecure youth with an unauthentic religious training and an equally unauthentic European polish, who goes abroad and longs for home, who is buffeted and wooed by multiple forces and whose development is truncated by internecine struggles — is an allegory for Argentina, whether or not this occurred to Mujica Láinez or to his compatriots.

III. «LOS CISNES»

Even before *Sergio* was in print, the novelist started a new book, which he completed in four months. It came out the following year, 1977, in a larger printing, indicative of the writer's increasing popularity. *Los cisnes* is even more Argentine than its predecessor; indeed, it is wholly *porteño*, focussing on Buenos Aires types, in a specific building downtown. One review of this work quite properly bears the title «El mundo en una casa».[10] That is, the run-down former mansion on Charcas Avenue is a veritable microcosm. It recalls, of course, *La casa*, on elegant Florida Street, but this time the novelist does not relate a family and building saga, but the intertwined lives of numerous tenants, most of whom do not even reside in the decaying landmark.

There is something allegorical about that «Palacio de los Cisnes», whose denizens occupy different levels — from the lowest, where a violent death occurs initially, to the penthouse, the scene of lofty endeavours and a poetic transfiguration. It is a Bohemian world of pseudo- and amateur artists, of which the reader got a glimpse in *Invitados en el Paraíso* and which had been little or never covered in Argentine literature, according to Villordo's review above. It is a segment of metropolitan society, which Mujica Láinez, as journalist and art critic, knows well and can describe

[10] By OSCAR HERMES VILLORDO, *La Nación*, 17 October 1977.

both with sympathy and satirical comment. As a matter of fact, he can appear himself in it and he does in this book as he did in others.

In *Los cisnes* he is the monocled art critic who comes to Leontina's exhibition. He also shows up at Niní's cocktail party, where he is buttonholed by the high priest of the Cubist sect, the object of his ridicule. In addition, the aged poet and central character, Aníbal, shares the writer's literary interests, as Nogales —the art expert of the famous newspaper— shares his professional experience. Moreover. the narrator, who uses the first person plural and calls himself «biógrafo del Palacio cisneo»,[11] unmistakably is the novelist himself, who frequently and ironically intrudes, offers background data, and turns to the reader with an old-fashioned «Quien nos lee» (147).

Mujica Láinez's aesthetic concern with swans, one of the facets of his Neo-Modernism, appeared already in *Los ídolos*. In the novel of 1977 the graceful birds of myth and legend are everywhere: in the title, the cover design, and epigraph (from a poem by W. B. Yeats); in the décor of the old building, which got its name from the ubiquitous swan motif; in the theme of Aníbal's interminable magnum opus, a universal anthology of swan poetry —another idolatry?— and in the poet's sensing the mysterious presence of flapping wings; last but not least, in the lexical abundance of Spanish slang, in which the word for swan also denotes «whore». Indeed, the Bohemian men and women of the «Palace of the Swans» engage in such shifting and ambiguous sexual alliances, that the latter make up the plot and the book title also refers to the characters.

The old building is the scene of nearly all episodes. The time of the novel spans only a couple of seasons typical of the River Plate climate. Historically, the re-emergence of Mimi Sergent —the culture hostess from *Sergio,* at the grotesque wedding of the dilettante heiress Niní with the hustler Efraín— suggests that *Los cisnes* is likewise contemporary. However, there are no political allusions; only the disintegration of modern *porteño* society is quite obvious.

The novel's episodes are structured in ten chapters, which bear ironic titles: e.g. III, «Homenaje a Eurípides», relates an experimental theater performance in a garage which burns down. The book opens with the old poet at work; it ends with his death and wake, attended by all the characters, thus affording a sum-up as Mujica Láinez is wont to provide. Its last paragraphs, evoking similar apotheoses in the writer's biographical works, suggests swans carrying aloft Aníbal's soul, although seen only by a few pure-at-heart. This produces a poetic and hopeful final note for a series of tales of egotism, sham, and lust, held together by their location.

---

[11] MANUEL MUJICA LÁINEZ, *Los cisnes* (Buenos Aires, 1977), p. 133. This work, too, will be cited in the text by page number.

The beginning of the book is interrupted by an outcry — another of the writer's constants. The tenants hardly know each other; in the end they form a group, albeit marginal, of related artistic talent or pretensions. Beyond that looms the destruction of the quaint edifice, likely to make room for a more profitable one. Thus Mujica Láinez again registers the passing of the old Buenos Aires.

Whereas the Percival-like Sergio is destroyed at the close of the preceding book, *Los cisnes* begins with the death of a youth Damián, whose spectral presence is felt later, as was the one of Tristán, in *La casa*. *Los cisnes*, however, is dominated by one Efraín, who is startlingly handsome but the exact opposite of the dreamy Sergio. Efraín, the bisexual gigolo, serves as a catalyst in the novel. He is a nobody, whose antecedents are deliberately left blank by the writer, but who ends up marrying the wealthy dilettante Niní. His sexual entanglements intertwine the various plot lines and also lead to the dénouement. He is not a major character, though, at least not one developed in any way.

The two penthouse occupants, on the other hand, rank among Mujica Láinez's best creations. Discounting the Spanish janitor, they are the only renters that sleep in the old mansion. Aníbal is a retired high school teacher of French and English whose sole interest is the swan theme in literature. For his anthology in the making, he produces Spanish versions of foreign poems on the topic. This enables the writer to include translations, which apparently are his own, and to discuss literature. Therefore, selections from Prudhomme, Mallarmé, Yeats, Darío, etc., are not at all out of place in *Los cisnes*. But it is the old poet's candor and warmth which endears him to the other personages and to the reader. He befriends especially Leontina, the other lonely, rooftop dweller, and her cat. Leontina is an aging prostitute, a kind soul, who assists the frail septuagenarian. She too has a strange hobby; she likes to draw and her inspiration comes from an old Bible. When one of her mature customers sees these pictures, he instantly recognizes them as «primitive painting» and, being an influential critic, arranges for an exhibition. The successful show and Leontina's following marriage to the critic Nogales are events which the writer can relate with glee.

However, Leontina and Aníbal are not the butt of Mujica Láinez's satire. They are treated with a tenderness and compassion which border on the lyrical. The other denizens of the Swan Palace border on caricatures, even when they are portrayed with understanding. With the exception of the vulgar partners in a picture-framing business (who provide a totally different perspective) all are frustrated artists with high aspirations and, mostly, shaky finances. They cultivate a variety of arts and show —or hide— various sexual preferences. Unlike *Sergio*, here homosexuality becomes the butt of the novelist's satire.

There is the sculptor Miguel, who is supported by his uncle, a retired bishop. Miguel likes boys for his models. When a statue crushes Damián, at the start, the scandalized tenants blame his rival Efraín for the accident. The despondent sculptor eventually kills himself. Then the ancient prelate's grief and the devotion of his old housekeeper, her call at the palace of iniquity, and the return visit of the tenant Morgana —almost leading to the latter's conversion— make up the best side show in the book.

Teresio Morgana is a producer of experimental theater which does not go beyond the rehearsal stage — except the Euripides play, which becomes a fiery fiasco. After the Greek drama he tries one by Musset and he considers one by Claudel. He, too, likes young males, who are his constantly changing stars. These actors hold the most prosaic jobs in the city and the account of the entire operation is a clever satire on a sector of the theater in Buenos Aires, of which I have some personal knowledge. Mujica Láinez's perdurable interest in the dramatic genre is seen also in a couple of gossipy (and inaccurate) commentaries on the building's scandals, which are printed in the form of scenes, with heightened comical effect.

The painter Calzetti is another pathetic character, who makes an austere cult of passé Cubism and tries to hide his latent homosexuality. One of his «novices» abandons him to nurse Aníbal, with the help of Leontina, in the poet's last days. However, the most complex of the shifting alliances, which are essential to the plot, are the betrayals by Efraín. He switches from the sculptor to the producer and then takes up with Niní. Also, he gets involved with both a male and a female dancer, for there is a dance studio on the premises. The elderly lady who teaches Spanish dances accepts a ballet student, since she comes with a wealthy sponsor who can subsidize a recital. Noëmi, a voluptuous Jewish divorcée and mistress of a mature Jewish jeweller, wants to perform, naturally, «The Death of the Swan». She is easily seduced by Efraín. Their lovemaking, in the furniture storage section of the old mansion, is perhaps the only case of unlabored, passionate, heterosexual relations in the works of Mujica Láinez. Their discovery, during Niní's reception, affords a grotesque tableau.

Niní and her associate, María Teresa, are the «stylish señoritas» of the palace. Aristocratic dilettantes, they can afford to pay to have their products exhibited and reviewed at home and abroad. María Teresa marries an industrialist who dabbles in abstract painting; Niní «acquires» Efraín. The building's «poor señoritas» eke out an existence painting horoscopes and imparting spiritual force through Yoga. It is one of the ironies of these Bohemian tales that the ailing Aníbal does not benefit from the Yoga session. Rather he falls gravely ill and his death marks the end of the book and of the association of curious but recognizable social types. Some are stereotypes, such as Mujica Láinez's Jews (like the blacks in earlier works), but all are plausible and intensely human. Indeed, there is something universal about these Bohemians of Buenos Aires.

The novelist's vision clearly mellowed a lot in his more recent works of Argentine setting. Villordo's review rightly calls it an «óptica» of «lo humorístico y lo poético». *Los cisnes* is also a compendium of the writer's tried motifs and techniques, which do not have to be re-enumerated. However, it seems appropriate to cite some examples of his best satirical prose. Of the Cubists he says:

> Estos adoraban a Calzetti y Calzetti adoraba al Cubo. El Cubo era su dios. Fuera del Cubo, cuyos seis cuadrados iguales encerraban las Tablas de la religión verdadera, el resto no pasaba de un amasijo de idolatrías, herejías, apostasías, libertinajes y ateísmos. Y Leonardo Calzetti circulaba, sacerdote magno de una secta extinguida, de una liturgia sobreviviente en el seno de esa ermita postrera, entre aquellos que, de pie frente a sus caballetes como ante pequeños altares, reiteraban con devoción, año tras año, los mismos arlequines, las mismas naturalezas muertas, muertas por la indigestión constante de esferas, de conos, de cilindros y, naturalmente, de cubos. (45f)

And he calls the janitor «Cerbero, graduado en escobas, escobillones, plumeros y cepillos, pero desdeñoso de uso, y depositario circunstancial (por curiosidad, indiscreciones y cercanía) de secretos vislumbrados, que constituyen la parte 'amateur' y más significativa de su personalidad porteril» (62). Here belong also the enumeration of nine Spanish synonyms for prostitute (107) and its untranslatable, in part, neologistic, extension: «la gran puta, reputa, reputona, reputaña, reputísima, colmo de la reputería reputesca» (119).

With his *Los cisnes* Mujica Láinez has given a new twist to the artist-protagonist of Modernist fiction. Its characters are not authentic artists; they can be added to the gallery of inauthentic personages in his previous works, going all the way back to the idolaters of his «Saga». They are not the victims of constant disillusion, as are the protagonists of the historical novels; rather, they suffer from self-delusion, but their story is well told with a smiling understanding.

IV. «EL GRAN TEATRO»

After *Los cisnes* Mujica Láinez did not produce another novel for two years. He did publish a collection of short stories, *El brazalete y otros cuentos,* in 1978, but they had appeared in periodicals long before. Their place in the writer's works will be discussed in the following chapter. The 1979 novel, *El gran teatro,* is laid in the period in which Mujica had begun to publish extensively, the pre-Perón era in Argentina. The setting is the Buenos Aires of 1942, a little before the historic time of *Invitados en el Paraíso,* the end of World War II and the dissolution of the country's high society. The background of *El gran teatro* is the turning point of that war, as neutral Argentina, at the time of the battle of Stalingrad, manoeuvred between the Allies and the Axis, and the great society, though slightly wilted, still showed elements of splendor. This setting inspires the plot and provides the subject for conversation and interior monologues.

In the same interview,[12] in which the writer conceded that he could not vouch for the authenticity of his portrayal of the Middle Ages in his *Unicornio*, he attested to the accuracy of his description of life in Buenos Aires in *El gran teatro*. There is no reason to doubt this. The new novel is more than a homecoming; it is the real finale for the Saga of Buenos Aires, not only because of the dramatic connotation of the title. This also confirms my conception of *Invitados en el Paraíso* as an epilogue. The fact that one of the rival matriarchs of the 1979 novel is a classmate of Duma, the grande dame of the Saga books, merely stresses the link to the earlier works.

The author claims that, although he needed only half of the year 1978 to write *El gran teatro*, it took him twice as long to document it. It required a detailed knowledge of the layout and the décor of the city's opera house and of the most elegant ladies' fashions at the time. Indeed, the book is a good indication that Mujica Láinez, the creator of numerous striking male characters, is equally capable of portraying feminine beauty, which may have added to the novel's success with readers of both sexes. It had not only an initial Argentine printing of ten thousand copies but a separate edition in Spain, almost simultaneously. Included in the vast collection of Mujica Láinez anecdotes is the information that, after the publication of the three historical novels in Spain and television appearances in Madrid, the writer was invited to the palace to present *El gran teatro* to the King. The book may reach an even wider audience in future, if the project of a costly film materializes.

The novel takes place in the Teatro Colón, in 1942 still one of the world's three or four great opera centers. In addition to the dramatic unity of space, Mujica Láinez also observed the unity of time, i.e. the span of one performance of Wagner's *Parsifal*. (This is followed by a one-page Epilogue with a surprise ending.) One could also speak of a unity of action, because the plot really is the sum total of the numerous subplots. There is constant switching from stage to house and from one subplot to the other, amidst the dazzling splendor of the setting, which almost suggests a movie script.

The three-hundred-page volume shows on its cover the proscenium of the famous theater and, inside, a colored photo of the writer in its Golden

---

[12] With MARÍA SÁENZ QUESADA, *Clarín*, 10 January 1980.

Hall. The book is dedicated to Alberto Ginastera, the composer of the *Bomarzo* opera, and to two others. The epigraphs, appropriately taken from Wagner and Heine, refer to opera-goers. Whereas Heine's audience goes to see rather than to hear the opera, Mujica Láinez's obviously goes to be seen. This is why in the novel's five major divisions, which correspond to those of the performance, the Intermissions have equal or greater importance than the three acts of the long opera. As a matter of fact, the «Primer Entreacto» is the book's longest section. There is also a substantial introductory «Entrada» and a brief «Salida» section, plus the «Epílogo». Thus, even structurally, the preeminence of the audience over Wagner's liturgical pageant is clear. The academician González Lanuza appropriately entitled the review of his colleague's book «Cuando el personaje es el público», and he considered the opera performance merely a screen to receive the projection of the tragical and farcical happenings in the various levels of the house.[13]

These happenings, many of which only occur in the minds of the characters, are related by an omniscient narrator, not separate from the writer, who calls himself a chronicler,[14] but who occasionally intrudes into the action. Sometimes his inspiration in contemporary reality is transparent, as when he says of a lady «... nos recuerda rasgos psicológicos propios de su padre...» (72). One has the impression that the novelist knows well the prototypes of all the characters that appear in *El gran teatro*. And many they are! Although I have shied away from a census of characters in Mujica Láinez's fiction, a quick count in the 1979 book is quite astonishing. There are two thousand five hundred people at the opera house (compared to a giant, gilded bird cage), whose movements are likened to rivers. Of these spectators the writer singles out twenty, whom we might call major characters, since their actions and aspirations seem essential to the basic plot. Their development may be uneven and often slight. Yet there are twenty even lesser ones whose mini-plots contribute to the panoramic vision of the end of an era. They range from the guests in the presidential box to the students in the top gallery.

All belong to the upper or middle class and only a few of the forty work for a living. Their presence at the performance of the difficult *Parsifal* is largely due to social pressures and considerations. It is obvious that the German conductor despises his affluent, not genuinely cultured audience and also that the old Hispanic aristocracy looks down on the newcomers that are infiltrating and about to replace it. This is the background of the multiple plot lines, which are effectively manipulated by the novelist. He even takes pride in having set up a vast comedy of intrigues in which,

---

[13] *La Nación*, 26 August 1979.
[14] MANUEL MUJICA LÁINEZ, *El gran teatro* (Buenos Aires, 1979), p. 198. Further quotations by page number in the text.

for the first time, he causes characters or groups to act independently, while they are linked by an overall entanglement, of which they themselves are not aware.[15]

Indeed, the opposing octogenarians, María and Amelia, never meet face to face. The feuding cousins head different branches of the same aristocratic clan: Amelia's, still immensely rich, María's —unbeknown to society— on the brink of bankruptcy. The former is not feeling well, but plans to give a ball in honor of her granddaughter, the Number One Heiress in town. The supreme goal of nearly all the major and minor characters (and the essence of most subplot lines) is to be invited to the ball or to be connected with it in some way. In the book's ironic one-page epilogue, which describes Amelia's solemn funeral (reminiscent of that of another Latin American matriarch[16]) we learn the ball never took place.

An integral part of the main plot is María's design to avert financial collapse through a marriage of her grandson Alejandro to the daughter of the vulgar Capris, the new landowners of Italian descent. To achieve this, the girl, too, needs an invitation to Amelia's ball. Add to this the display of a priceless heirloom, the necklace of a vicereine of Perú, which María is wearing and which is known to be the cause of her feud with Amelia. But this is just one of the countless false assumptions, illusions, and delusions, which Mujica Láinez serves up in this book. The necklace is no longer what it was, since its priceless gems have largely been replaced by fake stones, as only the distinguished (of course, Jewish) jeweller notes. And the necklace had only been a pretext; the real cause of their rivalry was that Amelia's husband had been discovered with María decades ago. During the *Parsifal* performance the ailing Amelia would like to forgive her cousin, to make up, but the reconciliation —like the dance— never comes about.

This comedy of manners —in great part comedy of errors— of Buenos Aires society shows more suspense than any of the writer's works since *Invitados en El Paraíso*. The «Great Theater» clearly is not the Teatro Colón, but the theater of life, of the world, in the Calderonian sense. González Lanuza, in the aforementioned review, even considered Mujica Láinez's title to be a pun and he labelled the novel, in a parody of Calderón's «Gran teatro del mundo» a «Teatro del gran mundo».

Now, this world of (mostly) beautiful and elegant people is shown by the writer to have considerable style but to be a sad one. All those who are scrambling for invitations, favors, love, or recognition are essentially lonely, insecure, and eventually defeated, as are most of the novelist's characters. Some, at times, are stirred by Wagner's music and scenes.

---

[15] See the interview with Luis Antonio de Villena, «Mujica Láinez entre la literatura y la vida», *Insula*, 34, Nos. 392-93 (1979), 1.
[16] «Los funerales de Mamá Grande», by Gabriel García Márquez.

The development of *Parsifal,* with its themes, motives, and staging —which are detailed by Mujica Láinez— parallels or contrasts with their private dramas, so as to give the impression that it is the great opera which orchestrates their small lives. Many of them are stock characters, several only caricatures, albeit striking ones. A few in Mujica's gilded bird cage —one is tempted to call it a zoo— are rather well developed and unusual ones in his vast census of personages.

There is the lanky Salvador, recently arrived from the country, a handsome youth who rejects homosexual advances, specifically those of his fallen idol, uncle Alejandro, who is a failure as a pederast but is expected to marry Tina Capri. Perhaps the best characterization is that of the pompous professor and literary scholar (Mujica Láinez makes fun of us) from Argentina's interior, who intrudes on everybody and is referred to only as the Toad, which creature he resembles. This is merely one of many zoomorphic labels that appear in *El gran teatro.* The opposing factions of Francophiles and Germanophiles in the audience are headed by the Mouse (Mlle. Truc, of the French Institute) and Hawk (the visiting prince from Hitler Germany). Then there are not very marriageable sisters, called the Seals, whereas the most heavily bedecked ladies are called Birds. The crowds in search of refreshments, during intermission time, are Ants, etc. Another satirical technique, stressed in the novel, is the use of epithets: e.g. the lovely music fan who is following the score is always «The Lady with the Flashlight», but the Heiress' retarded sister is merely «The Mongoloid».

Among a number of caricatures stand out the obese matron which aerostatic breasts who munches bonbons throughout the performance and the distinguished visitors from England. The latter may well be the best odd but amazingly real types created by the novelist. Sir Francis, «Turtle Gregory», [sic] has pursued and studied turtles (with subspecies enumerated by Mujica Láinez) all over the world and

> ha terminado por convertirse en una tortuga más, lo cual es, probablemente, el ideal del auténtico herpetólogo. Ahora Sir Francis se interesa por las tortugas argentinas. Sobre todo por *una* tortuga. Y lo hace con el fervor que consagra el tema, y que le ensancha más aún la boca, le torna más separados y vítreos los ojos, le alarga y frunce todavía más el cuello; en una palabra, lo vuelve más tortuga, tanto que en un momento así cabe sosopechar que de las escamas de la giba que le abulta la espalda, se pueden sacar láminas de carey, para fabricar peines, anteojos, nécessaires, etc. (235ff)[17]

The British scientist's immediate purpose is to prove an error in taxonomy, i.e. that the «Geochelone Chilensis» is really an Argentine turtle,

---

[17] In this connection one cannot help thinking of the Guatemalan Modernist RAFAEL ARÉVALO MARTÍNEZ's zoomorphic tales, e.g. *El hombre que parecía un caballo* (1914).

to the delight of the host government. Thus Mujica Láinez satirizes the border dispute between the two countries at the time of his writings.

Lady Gregory is a retired Shakespearean actress who has preserved the ruins of her beauty and career (as Cleopatra) by assuming an Egyptian air which earns her the epithet «Pharaonian». Her superstitious exclamation —another scream— linking a change of color in a ruby she is wearing to the imminent death of a woman is the only trace of the fantastic in the most realistic fiction the novelist has written.

Sex, in *El gran teatro,* is always present but greatly subdued. With the exception of Alejandro's fumbling, it is normal. There are affairs and lascivious thoughts —e.g. the seduction scene of the opera stimulates a small catalogue of dreams— but the motives of the vast number of characters are Adlerian rather than Freudian: they are complexes of inferiority and (false) superiority; they involve prestige and social status, which may include sexual status, rather than sex.

This is seen also in the dialogue passages, in which much is said that is thought differently. Some dialogues again appear in dramatic form, as the writer, in his opera novel, comes closer than ever to the theater. The scene in which Señor Capri visits María's box and the men talk simultaneously about livestock and Wagner could be from one of the early River Plate comedies.

The early twentieth-century flavor is quite pervasive in *El gran teatro.* There is something distinctly Modernist in the choice of a Wagnerian opera. So is the central position of the famous necklace and the insistence on the theater's lavish ornamentation and statuary. Persons and situations are seen in terms of pictures; the sheen of objects in the darkened house is stressed. Beautiful Eugenia is compared to a model of the Pre-Raphaelite painters. Here belong also the great entrance of the matriarchs and their respective retainers, as well as the hieratic exit of the ailing Amelia to her funereal Rolls Royce. But there are more than mere literary echoes in the book. Verlaine and Heine are cited verbatim and one student in the last row of gallery seats actually composes a poem, with the title «Parsifal», during the performance.

Still nothing, not even literature, escapes the sarcasm of Mujica Láinez. He says of the emasculated Klingsor's evil influence:

> Cayó Amfortas, el Rey, y de no haber caído, faltarían algunas mejores en el «Perceval» de Chrétien de Troyes y también en el «Perzival» de Wolfram von Eschenbach, fuente principal de Wagner, de modo que si Klingsor no se hubiera mudado, por mano propia, en un brujo capón, el «Parsifal» wagneriano no hubiera existido, ni tampoco el libro que el lector honra en este momento y que se funda en él, y, en consecuencia, tanto Wagner como quien esto escribe, le agradecen a Klingsor su decisión quirúrgica. (161)

Although *El gran teatro* brings to mind the famous dialect account of another Argentine opera performance —the gauchesque *Fausto,* by Estanislao del Campo, of 1866— Mujica Láinez's novel on the staging of Wagner's *Parsifal* in the Teatro Colón in 1942 markedly differs by its universality. In spite of all local detail and flavor, its vision of a society about to be eclipsed would hardly be different, were it to describe such a performance in the twilight of the Austrian or the British empire. González Lanuza's review called the author of *El gran teatro* a moralist in spite of himself. Indeed, in this novel Mujica Láinez has returned to the type of social satire[18] for which he was acclaimed in the 1950s.

V. «LOS PORTEÑOS»

There is nothing universal about *Los porteños*. It completes the author's homecoming and it is clearly a product for local consumption. A totally retrospective book, it contains no new material but exhibits a cultural heritage for the benefit of future generations. The 1979 volume may have been written also with a view to the city's coming quadricentennial. It is a medley of Mujica Láinez's non-fictional prose, assembled by him for a specialized publisher. (The publications of Librería de la Ciudad also include two other items under his signature, but those collections of artistic photos of places with accompanying text are non-literary, urban travel books.[19]) *Los porteños* is centered on people and, basically, an essay-type book. As such it is akin only to the writer's *Glosas castellanas* of 1936. Both are difficult to classify: *Glosas* has also fictional aspects, as we have seen; *Porteños* is heavily illustrated. It is really a celebration of roots.

The intent to exalt great figures of Buenos Aires is seen already in the format. *Los porteños* measures eight and half by twelve and a quarter inches, it is printed on art reproduction paper and its cover is a collage of fourteen photos of famous Porteños, with the writer in the center. The hundred and eighty-two pages are interspersed with one hundred and four illustrations, showing individuals or groups, paintings, and interiors, all from Mujica Láinez's own large collections, now housed at «El Paraíso». The luxurious looking volume is, obviously, destined for the coffee table trade.

Its variegated content is interesting, because the writer's tastes and

---

[18] This aspect is stressed by Jorge Campos in his review of Mujica's novel (*Insula*, 398 [1980]), but the Spanish critic thinks also of Proust, Calderón, and *El diablo cojuelo*. Parallels between Vélez de Guevara and Mujica Láinez merit further exploration.
[19] *Letras e imágenes de Buenos Aires* (1976) and *Más letras e imágenes de Buenos Aires* (1978), photos by Aldo Sessa.

opinions, thus far, have been noted only indirectly, through his fictional works. The book is divided into thirty-one selections.[20] They were written in the forty-year span of 1939 to 1979 and include articles, speeches, obituaries, and prologues — even one that could be termed a commercial. Yet all concern remarkable individuals or their mementos. With a few exceptions, they had been published previously, mostly in *La Nación*. Some selections are even taken from Mujica's books.

In spite of their heterogeneity in format and style, the *Porteños* items have something in common beyond the subject matter. They are journalistic but carefully written personal reactions to an individual, to his setting, to a situation, or to an event. These happen to be also the characteristics of the Modernist Chronicle of the turn of the century and one could label the writer's last book a collection of «crónicas». They may have the format of a «semblanza» (a profile or character sketch) or an obituary; they may describe a place or an object of artistic or historical significance. In style, the selections of *Los porteños* range from an eloquent praise of the city, through a formal lecture and an informal dialogue, to a plain prologue of a company publication (on the history of the Bullrich firm, instrumental in the agricultural development of the Republic). They vary also greatly in length.

Together these selections reaffirm the cultural roots of the country. Mujica Láinez calls it a «petite histoire», since it deals with people and places past, rather than great events. Some of the places no longer exist or have become museums, but *Los porteños* is not another book of internal tourism. Even the nine final items, entitled collectively «La historia viva en nuestras casas tradicionales», are evocations of the surroundings of great men, in some cases those of figures sketched before. Among the profiles of people of artistic bent stand out those of Larreta and of Victoria Ocampo.

It will surprise no one that the Porteños appearing in the volume are largely interrelated and, in many cases, even related to Mujica Láinez. One selection states that the old families can easily be traced back to the founder of the city, Juan de Garay; another «La historia patria y la de nuestras viejas familias están tan enlazadas, que son inseparables».[21] At least ten items concern the writer's ancestors; others, too, have autobiographical aspects. This is especially interesting since Mujica Láinez never wrote an autobiography.

In the evocation of the men that built the country and of those that later enriched it culturally one can discern a strong racial pride, some-

---

[20] They are really thirty-nine, since the last had originally appeared in nine independent instalments over a period of seven months.
[21] MANUEL MUJICA LÁINEZ, *Los porteños* (Buenos Aires, 1979), p. 71. This book also will be cited within the text by page number only.

thing previously obfuscated by the irony and satire of the writer's fiction. *Los porteños* stresses the Hispanic qualities of Argentina's former leaders. They are seen as a closely-knit bourgeois aristocracy, landed or monied, which co-opted a few foreigners from Britain and the continent.

Mujica Láinez's Porteños appear very anglophile. They are independently wealthy —if not fantastically rich— and always eager to acquire artistic treasures abroad. One of them, Juan Cruz Varela II, so crammed his sumptuous residence that he had to auction off periodically part of his collections in order to continue his acquisitions. Most of these men had eclectic tastes, but some were real connoisseurs and the country owes much of its cultural patrimony to their efforts.

Whereas the Porteños of *Los porteños* amassed artistic treasures rather than objects of conspicuous consumption —as do some of the writer's snobbish fictional characters— all seem to show a lack of concern for the land and the people that produced and managed the wealth which enabled them to make these acquisitions. Therefore, one can understand better some of the criticism levelled against this oligarchy and also the later rise of Peronism. *Los porteños* extols a magnificent cultural elite. Intertextual links to Mujica's preceding or following fictional works, are quite apparent: e.g. the opera house, the villa on the river bank, the mansion on Florida Street, and the Swan Palace are found also in this non-fiction book.

Literary historians will be interested in lists of mid-nineteenth-century readings in «La biblioteca de Florencio Varela» and in the autographed entries by contemporary authors in an album of Miguel Cané's first wife «Los proscriptos en un álbum de 1846». The only other reference to the dictatorship of Rosas is found in the opening selection, «Esta Buenos Aires», which sees the city overcoming both «el primer tirano» and «el segundo» (11). The second, of course, is Perón, who did not permit the Society of Authors to honor a Mexican philosopher in a public ceremony («Una medalla para Francisco Romero»).

The most significant items in this uneven volume appear in its initial and closing selections. The book opens with the aforementioned «Esta Buenos Aires», a lyrical declaration of love for the great city, which brings to mind the words of the tango Mujica Láinez had written in the 1960s. He calls Buenos Aires the «Ciudad Elegida», the «Ciudad de la Nostalgia» (12). This is followed by a dialogue with another great Porteño, Jorge Luis Borges. In «El amor por Buenos Aires» the two writers discuss the role of the city in their work, but, in essence, make light of serious matters.

They are not joking, however, when Mujica Láinez calls it an advantage that in Buenos Aires everything was still to be done, whereas in London and Paris everything had already been done; or when Borges considers the Argentines more European than the Europeans; «nosotros somos herederos de toda la cultura occidental, no tenemos por qué fijarnos en una región más que en otra. Somos lo que queremos y podamos ser» (15). They agree that the Argentine's desire to return to Europe stems from a feeling of exile (18). The two friends also agree that their sources of the region's primitive past are in part apocryphal or hearsay.

Nevertheless, it is the past which forms the colophon of *Los porteños*. Mujica Láinez evokes the atmosphere of the Láinez residence of old and in the Modernist prose of many of his final paragraphs, he imagines elegant ladies of the time who «se arrebujan en las capas de armiño y de marta y avanzan majestuosas, hacia los extranjeros célebres que les besarán las manos» (182).

6

LAST WORKS

In the last years of his life Mujica Láinez not only produced two new fictional works, but also had the satisfaction of seeing a dozen books published which made previous writings available to a much broader audience. (This count does not include the reprinting in Spain of Saga novels, back to *Los ídolos,* of the historical trilogy, and even the Shakespearean sonnets.) One of these twelve volumes was a collection of short stories written in the previous decade. In view of their literary merit and their possible links to the major works of the author, they will be discussed in some detail below after brief observations on the other miscellaneous publications of recent years. Then we shall examine Mujica's nineteenth fictional work, *El escarabajo,* which became a best seller in Spain. Also the last, *Un novelista en el Museo del Prado,* published only a few weeks before the writer's death, on 21 April 1984. It has been reported that on his desk was the plan for a new book, on a nineteenth-century Argentine topic. Thus after two further universalist works and wide acclaim in Europe, Mujica Láinez returned once more to his country's past, at a time when Argentina rediscovered her democratic traditions.

I. Miscellaneous Publications

The series *Obras completas,* initiated in 1978 by Editorial Sudamericana, reached Volume V by 1983, with the last of the Saga novels and the art book «Victorica», obviously minus its plates. The continuation of this monumental publishing project, even in competition with Mujica's latest books, at a time of severe economic stress, was a sure sign of the author's enduring popularity at home, although he was largely ignored by academic criticism.[1]

---

[1] See e.g. the special issue of *Revista Iberoamericana* devoted to forty years of Argentine literature, which alludes to Mujica Láinez only in one line and a footnote (1983), 957.

A collection of six items, culled from *Aquí vivieron, Misteriosa Buenos Aires, Crónicas reales, Cecil, El viaje de los siete demonios,* and the aforementioned *El brazalete y otros cuentos,* appeared in 1981 under the title *El poeta perdido y otros relatos*.[2] The selection was Jorge Cruz's, who also provided a brief prologue with emphasis on Mujica's pictorial and prosopopeia techniques.

Páginas de Manuel Mujica Láinez seleccionadas por el autor, published the following year,[3] is a very different and more extensive collection, with a substantial introduction by Oscar Hermes Villordo. The book is made up of materials dispersed in periodicals over the decades and to all effects unavailable. These short items are most varied and they illustrate the writer's likes and dislikes, his journalistic pursuits, and his penchant for occasional poetry. They include lectures and speeches, verbal portraits, both in prose and in verse —clearly a Modernist subgenre— sample translations, and lesser regional travel chronicles. We even find the text of the «Bomarzo Cantata», not accessible before. This material, mostly undated, gives an indication of the variety of Mujica's circumstantial writings, of an earlier tendency toward the rhetorical, but also of a progression toward a limpid language. It may not have occurred to him that he was referring to his own mature style when he called Larreta, at the inauguration of the monument in his honor, «maestro del pulcro decir» (122). The facility of expression, the ironic tone, the love of word play, and the emphasis on things Hispanic are present already in Mujica's earliest products.

Not yet included in any collection are a few short items which Mujica wrote in his last years: «El coleccionista de caracoles», a new version of the motif of a person's projection into an object; also a commemoration of Gerchunoff and of a society lady who may have been a model for the Mimi Sergent of *Sergio*.[4] In the twilight of the military regime, the writer, an inoffensive, picturesque remnant of earlier days, became a favorite of the media. This did not stop him from speaking out against censorship in an interview.[5]

One of the belated great satisfactions was the publication of his beloved *El unicornio* in the English-speaking world under the title *The Wandering Unicorn,* also in 1982.[6] Translated by Mary Fitton and encomiastically prefaced by Borges,[7] it was extremely well received in

---

[2] (Buenos Aires, 1981), 113 pp., Biblioteca Argentina Fundamental.
[3] (Buenos Aires, 1982), 233 pp.
[4] *La Nación,* 21 November 1982; 18 September and 31 December 1983, respectively.
[5] «Un hombre del renacimiento», *Clarín,* 25 March 1982, signed by Juan Bedoian.
[6] Toronto, 1982; London, 1983; New York, 1983.
[7] According to BORGES, «Manuel Mujica Láinez brings back to contemporary

England. The *Times Literary Supplement* compared it to *Cien años de soledad* and noted that Mujica «observes medieval life, high and low, with an irony that cuts straight through any conventional glamour».[8] Anthony Burgess called the book a reminder that Spanish American fiction is not just *Cien años de soledad* and he concluded: «But Láinez will never get the Nobel; he writes too well and there is no political protest in him.»[9] Several British reviewers stressed the fairy-tale and tapestry effects of the book and the narratorial skill of its author. American criticism was likewise favorable, but the *New York Times* failed to note the novel's irony and confused its timing and protagonists.[10]

A useful addition to the writer's limited bibliography of secondary sources is *El mundo de Manuel Mujica Láinez: Conversaciones con María Esther Vázquez*, of 1983.[11] These somewhat chatty interviews offer insights —already occasionally quoted here— on the author's views of his own books and on his work habits. Much of this had appeared previously in magazines and other media: how he accumulates data about places and motifs in a series of black notebooks; how he composes in longhand in the morning hours and, after a nap, types an improved text, never to make further changes. *El mundo de Manuel Mujica Láinez* also contains the first authorial remarks on *El escarabajo,* published the same year in Spain. «Páginas del Diario de *El escarabajo*» might be considered a journal to accompany a ledger of black notebooks used in the elaboration of a book which, as we shall see, required considerable research.

Mujicas' latest collection, *Placeres y fatigas de los viajes,* presents itself as «Crónicas de viaje aparecidas en *La Nación* 1935-1977». I am unable to vouch for its completeness, but it is clear that many of the writer's travel chronicles describe the settings of his universalist fictional works. Volume I (1983) is already out of print. II was issued in 1984.

II. «EL BRAZALETE Y OTROS CUENTOS»

Unlike *Crónicas reales, De milagro y de melancolías* and *El viaje de los siete demonios,* which might be termed linked novellas, the nine tales of the 1978 collection are totally independent, lacking even the common

---

writing the sense of destiny, of adventure with its hope and fears, the tradition of Stevenson, Hugo and —why not?— Ariosto». He concludes: «The *Wandering Unicorn* is not a reconstruction of time past; it is like a glowing dream set in the past» (p. xi).

[8] COLIN GREENLAND, *TLS,* 22 April 1983.
[9] *Punch,* 27 April 1983.
[10] *New York Times Book Review,* 25 March 1984. The *Washington Post* had called *The Wandering Unicorn* a «gorgeous, rueful, and charming historical fantasy» (18 September 1983).
[11] (Buenos Aires, 1983), 212 pp. Colección Diálogos.

denominator of place, which characterized the writer's earlier collections *Aquí vivieron* and *Misteriosa Buenos Aires*. All seem to have been published previously. Most can be traced to *La Nación*, but one first appeared in Paris in a journal with broad Latin American diffusion.

El brazalete is a thin volume (one hundred and seventy pages), composed of stories of uneven length and quality; yet some are among Mujica Láinez's best. The publisher stressed their fantastic aspect, no doubt to promote sales, but this label is inaccurate, as we shall see. The book won a lesser award in 1979. It is dedicated to the writer's brother, a long-term resident of the United States. The location of the stories is quite varied. The title story is laid in Paris and Nice; the scene of the longest is Madrid and Toledo; that of the shortest is «the beyond». The rest take place in Argentina, one in the mountains of Córdoba. With the exception of the timeless post-mortem item and the peninsular story, laid in the age of *El laberinto,* the tales of *El brazalete* are strictly contemporary.

As the only grouping of unconnected stories of the writer, the collection is interesting from a number of angles. In most of the tales suspense is much stronger than in other narratives of the writer. Sex is minimal and it is entirely normal. In all but one the settings are interiors, but the luxury and splendor of old, of which we still got a glimpse in scenes of *Sergio* and one of *Los cisnes,* are absent. An ambience of decadence is strong in several stories, albeit without nostalgia. Objects: a mirror, a rare piece of jewelry, a painting, a manuscript, are central to the plots and, in a couple of instances, seem to have an animated existence. This enhances whatever fantastic aspect the 1978 volume has. A strong effect is attained also by the frequent use of a first-person, dramatized narrator who addresses a «you» (formal or informal Spanish you) to relate with realistic immediacy a totally unreal event. One story has the perspective of a female «I» quite different from the fairy Melusina of the preceding *El unicornio*.

«La viuda del Greco» tells her own story, which, though devoid of fantastic elements, is one of the best of the lot. As a maiden she meets the Greek painter who looks like his self-portrait. She marries the foreigner, because her father cannot arrange for her a more prestigious match. She moves to Toledo, but she does not like El Greco's house, his associates, nor his style of painting. She herself could never model for his elongated religious canvasses, which soon became commercialized art because of her husband's fame. She lives only for her son, Jorge Manuel, who models for the boy in his father's canvas «El entierro del Conde de Orgaz», and who also becomes a painter of sorts. His mother considers the youth's realistic, sensuous style superior to that of El Greco's. The ensuing power struggle during the artist's senility and, later, in the son's marriage is won by the mother. Yet she ends up an impoverished widow with a son who is a failure but to her is «el máximo pintor de Toledo».[12] In the psychology and the irony of this story Mujica Láinez is at his best. The slightly archaic language recalls that of the early *Glosas;* the setting is that of the future *Laberinto.* Indeed, the boy in the picture was to become that novel's protagonist.

Another case of delusion —which loomed so large in *Los cisnes*— is the unnamed lady of the brief «Importancias», who considers herself most important but after death finds that heaven is not waiting for her. So she stays, invisible, to experience her private hell in the realization of her total insignificance. This, to be sure, is more a morality tale than a short story. Nor should we consider fantastic her observing the «prolijas tareas sexuales» (68) of her heirs. But it is typical Mujica Láinez.

One story has an aura of fantasy, but the writer takes pain to suggest a rational explanation. «La larga cabellera negra» is a confession to a lady friend whom, after a party, he accompanied home. When she fell asleep, while he was reading Voltaire, he felt her tresses become alive and extend across the room to envelop and nearly choke him. He admits to having taken several whiskeys and to a routine Buenos Aires electric failure (but not the obvious Freudian interpretation of this sensuous dream or day-dream).

Three more tales have an eerie quality but seem more hallucinatory than fantastic. The book's opening story, «Narciso», is a third-person account of a strange recluse, who lives with numerous cats in a neglected apartment. He constantly stares at an old mirror, with the image of a striking youth staring back at him. He tries to keep the cats away, but when he dies the starving animals tear up everything, including the poster glued on the mirror. Mirrors and cats had fascinated Mujica Láinez before, but the new twist makes a good ending for a very brief story. In «Las alas» an elderly bachelor moves into an attic of a building decorated with winged figures. He is a newspaperman, a bitter critic, who still slaves on an (of course) interminable novel of his own. Sleepless, he hears sounds of big birds and flapping wings. In the end he floats the pages of his manuscript and jumps, joining the mysterious birds. This tale effectively combines the constants of journalism, the fatal leap, and of torn pages, but it foreshadows also the poetic aspect of *Los cisnes,* written years later.

The title story «El brazalete» seems completely realistic. It tells of an exiled queen, who could be a by-product of *Crónicas reales.* The old lady, who lives in Paris, may even be impoverished, but she wears a priceless bracelet of historical fame — including that of a curse on its wearer. At a sea-side hotel, where she is invited to attract customers, a

---

[12] MANUEL MUJICA LÁINEZ, *El brazalete y otros cuentos* (Buenos Aires, 1978), p. 63, henceforth to be cited within the text by page number.

hostile student tries to steal the famous piece from the bedroom of the sleeping queen. He has to give up when the jewel, in the form of a Crustacean, resists and pinches him. Only then he notices the queen's bared wrist and the cancerous scar which the bracelet had effectively hidden. If we discount the aggressively-protective animation of the jewel as a hallucination of the thief, «El brazalete» is just a tale with political, psychological, economic, and historical angles. It also recalls one of the Buenos Aires stories and an episode in the «Saga». Yet the tale may well be the germ of the biography of a famous jewel, *El escarabajo*.

This leaves three stories which might be termed fantastic. One was first printed in a science fiction anthology. «Los espías» takes place near the Argentine National Aerospace Research Institute. The writer tells his old friend Whitelow, by letter, of a strange vacation encounter. Among the few guests at his resort are the four obese Kohns, parents and teenage children. On a hike near the Institute, Mujica stumbles into the four fat strangers who are supine and seem lifeless. He is scared and even more so when four matching giant larvae enter the bodies via their mouths. He runs away, but the Kohn family never returns to the boarding-house. It is not explained whether these spongy Jews served as cocoons for worm-like international or inter-stellar observers. However, the confused tale clearly has a touch of old-fashioned anti-semitism and it is not surprising that it was not published in *La Nación*.

The remaining two are genuinely fantastic and, with their contrasting realistic setting, quite memorable. One takes place on city bus route 259, the other at a hippy pad. «El pasajero» purports to be the writer's personal experience on a rainy New Years's Eve, when he tries to return from downtown, laden with packages, to his Belgrano home. Finding no taxi, he takes a crowded bus. His attention is drawn to a fellow passenger, a youth. The latter rapidly ages on the trip and is dead of old age when Mujica, obviously shocked, reaches his destination. The quick glimpses of the stages of this metamorphosis, coinciding with the main points of the well known itinerary, amidst the indifference of the other riders, is skillfully orchestrated. The telescoping of a biological life span into a bus ride affords a fantastic story of the first order.

The setting of «El retrato» is an old house in an old neighborhood. A student lives there, the scion of an old family. His fellow students in the Humanities join him there to discuss strikes and literature and to make love. The casual atmosphere changes when the owner inherits a Renaissance painting of an unidentified master, supposedly the portrait of an architect, shown with the compass of his trade. The picture is felt to be spooky and the young people begin to stay away. The owner's girlfriend finally persuades him to sell the painting. When the dealer sends for it, the young man is found dead, with a neckwound caused by a vampire or a compass. Thereupon the old house deteriorates faster and soon crumbles into dust.

The most interesting aspect of this uneven volume, which is saved by the two fantastic tales and the El Greco story, is the insight it affords into Mujica Láinez's creative process. Several of these stories written between 1965 and 1970 seem to be by-products or previews of fictions on a larger scale.

III. «EL ESCARABAJO»

The belated success, in England and Spain, of *El unicornio,* which Mujica Láinez considers his most poetic work (*Mundo,* 101), proves that the writer correctly assessed the pulse of the time when he undertook the composition of another sophisticated, historical romance. It took him twenty-one months (1979-82) to produce *El escarabajo,* which is about the same size as the 1965 novel. Even before its completion, the rights had been acquired by Plaza y Janés, of Barcelona, with a large advance in dollars. The temporal and geographical coordinates of the new, decidedly universalist book are vast, exceeding even those of the fantastic *Viaje de los siete demonios.*

El escarabajo, the life story of the Scarab, spans the millennia from Ramses II to the days of the author. It is set mainly in the lands bounding the Mediterranean, with a definite stress on its eastern part — a zone favored by the Modernists. There is one British episode and a rather weak Argentinian one (no doubt a bow to Mujica's beloved city), but the Scarab's most striking adventures occur in Egypt, Greece, Asia Minor, Italy and at sea. The Egyptian Scarab itself is the book's first-person, dramatized narrator and, being an animated art object is, of course, immortal. We are dealing, therefore, with the autobiography of a gem. It is told to another work of art, a shipwrecked statue (both submerged), and finally dictated to the author.

There is a suggestion of a narrative frame —another Modernist favorite— since the book opens when the Jewel is flung into the sea by the Italian gigolo of an American millionairess but salvaged near the end. Within the frame the book returns to the past and the Scarab itself —the Winged Dung Beetle of ancient Egyptian mythology— is the symbol of «Eternal Return».[13]

The lapis lazuli Jewel had been fashioned by a magician for the wife of Ramses II, Queen Nefertari, who throughout the book symbolizes timeless beauty. It is interesting to note that the small Egyptian portion

---

[13] It has been noted before that Azorín, who cultivated this theme, had been a model for the young Mujica Láinez.

of Mujica's book, describing a Nile journey and a historic battle, parallels Norman Mailer's Egyptian novel *Ancient Evenings,* which became a bestseller in the United States in 1983. However, Mujica's book differs greatly from Mailer's monstruous seven hundred pages of repetitious mythology-cum-obscenity. Sex does pervade *El escarabajo,* but it is never obscene; it is lyrical, pathetic, even grotesque.

Whereas the American writer seems to have been bent on producing a masterpiece, the seventy-year-old Argentinian merely created a well-written synthesis of all his well-tried motifs and procedures. *El escarabajo* also reflects Mujica's concept of the essential sameness of humanity everywhere and at all times. His «I was there» technique is well suited for both this cosmovision and the traditional episodic structure.

The fate of the Jewel's transitory owners, who are all losers, and the lawful, criminal or accidental transfers of the gem make up the plot (or plots) of Mujica's work. The first transfer is clearly a violation of a tabu (desecration of a tomb). The Scarab then becomes involved with famous or unusual personages or in spectacular historical events and situations. Yet *El escarabajo* is not an historical novel but is steeped in history, cultural history, that is. Most of the characters are connected with the arts —another constant with Modernist writers— and most locations have an aura of refinement. These cultural heights are both nostalgically evoked and satirized.

The gem experiences one of its most memorable adventures when it is offered to Aristophanes by two courtesans with literary leanings. The Greek playwright, whose lines on winged beetles are cited, does not appreciate the gift. Later, in Rome, the Scarab witnesses Cesar's assassination. It belongs to one of the pious «Seven Sleepers of Ephesus», who is taken for a hippie. It accompanies Roland to his defeat at Roncesvalles. It is taken to Avalon. It appears in Marco Polo's Venice. It is connected with one of Michelangelo's beautiful male models and with one of the dwarfs of Velázquez's days. It is present at eighteenth-century séances —another Modernist concern we noted in Mujica's works— and it is owned by Sarah Bernhardt, and so forth.

The novelist has not only satirically recycled myth, art history, hagiography, and literature; he has even recycled an episode of one of his own best known creations: the unsuccessful seduction of the adolescent Duke of Bomarzo, of the opera and novel versions, by Pantasilea, is now seen from the perspective of her handsome Florentine page. We also re-encounter motifs such as the obese woman, travel, Mujica's tendency to recapitulate, and the ironic treatment of bourgeois wealth, science, even faith. All this is told in a mellow tone, with the use of a vast lexicon in descriptive passages alternating with very traditional Hispanic prose. An example of the latter (and of the persistence of human passions) is the Scarab's statement: «en la intimidad de mi mente escarabaja, de lo que cambia en el Mundo, son los proscenios y los actores, pero que del heredado palacio al hospedaje ruin, y de la Princesa de origen granado a la Posadera de tosca progenie, las escenas se repiten..., se repiten..., se repiten... sin que, no obstante, el Mundo merezca llamarse monótono.»[14]

The biography of the Scarab is anything but monotonous. It is full of surprises, coincidence, and chance, as is life; even the author's own life, about which he says, in connection with the aforementioned sale of *El escarabajo,* «¡como prueban esas mudanzas, esas apariciones de personajes inesperados, que todo lo que nos rodea y ocurre, es el fruto de un gran novelista creador! ¿Será una blasfemia llamar Dios así?» (*Mundo,* 204). Although Mujica has played God in the Scarab's progress through history, he has not made world history into a novel, as he thought he might.[15] The book's cover labels it a novel, but the critics do not agree on its classification. The Argentinian Noel called it an «expresión renovada de la novela histórica» and his review is entitled «Una magna gesta novelística».[16] His colleague, in *Clarín,* insists «es necesario, ante todo, no considerarlo una novela».[17] For Blas Matamoro *El escarabajo* seems «la más ambiciosa de las últimas novelas del autor».[18] MacAdam simply calls it «a text — not a novel but a wonderful exploration of aesthetics».[19] I consider *El escarabajo* as much a series of linked tales as a novel and, structurally, the work is related to the author's *Aquí vivieron, Crónicas reales,* and *El viaje de los siete demonios.*

This book places Mujica Láinez within the time-honored tradition of the Arabic frame narrative. A definition of the «Qasida» genre, recently applied to *Kalilah e Dimnah,* the *Decameron,* and the *Canterbury Tales,* also perfectly describes *El escarabajo:* «In a qasida, usually written in the first person, the speaker claims that he has either witnessed or actually experienced everything he describes. He often heightens the authenticity of his account by using names of real places and persons and depicting small details... Furthermore a qasida always contains elements of travel, of change, of motion... The episodes... are linked not by theme or location, but by a single point of view — that of the speaker who describes them».[20]

---

14 Manuel Mujica Láinez, *El escarabajo* (Barcelona, 1982), p. 305.
15 During the gestation of the book the author wrote that he was fascinated by a topic «which threatens to make world history into a novel». (Letter to George O. Schanzer, dated February 4, 1979.) Mujica's idea of God as a great novelist brings to mind Huidobro's concept of the poet as a «pequeño dios».
16 Martín Alberto Noel, *La Nación,* 23 May 1982.
17 «Real y aterradora», by Liliana Heker, *Clarín,* 22 July 1982.
18 B. M., «Entrelíneas», *Cuadernos Hispanoamericanos,* 385 (julio 1982), 238-40.
19 Alfred J. MacAdam, *World Literature Today,* 57 (1983), 433.
20 Katherine Slater Gittes, «*The Canterbury Tales* and the Arabic Frame Tradition», *PMLA,* 98 (1983), 241ff.

That view point is Mujica's constant irony, which the *Cuadernos Hispanoamericanos* review, cited above, finds in the book's «juego de permanencia y transitoriedad». The most succint summation, as well as a most balanced and favorable view of the best-selling work, is the one already noted, in *World Literature Today:* «Why do we bother to read Mujica Láinez? His prose is hopelessly old-fashioned, his vocabulary rarified, his thematics 'irrelevant' to contemporary concern. *El escarabajo* is the best answer imaginable to these foolish questions.» In continuation MacAdam calls it «a tour of art history and human passion». He concludes: «Like its author, this text holds fast to certain traditional values: we may disagree with them, but we must respect them, particularly when they produce a work as genial as this one.»

The brevity of this review, in conformity with the standards of the widely-read journal, may explain why the acute MacAdam did not identify the author's old-fashionedness and traditional values simply as «Modernist». However, one wonders why the critic, who had correctly labeled much of Spanish American narrative as satire,[21] did not point out the satire in Mujica Láinez's *El escarabajo* where it constitutes its modernity and one of the bases of its unusual success.

IV. «UN NOVELISTA EN EL MUSEO DEL PRADO»

After *El escarabajo* Mujica Láinez became a favorite of the news media in Spain also and it is not surprising that the former Secretary of the Museo de Arte Decorativo de Buenos Aires and art critic of *La Nación* was asked to produce a Spanish television series on the Prado Museum. The project did not materialize and, on his return to Argentina, Anita suggested the short story be used as a vehicle for the subject.[22] Thus the twelve linked tales which make up Mujica's last work were born. No. 643 of the «Biblioteca Breve» of Seix Barral is a slim volume, in the good company of products of the pens of Musil, Faulkner, Paz, Hemingway, Kundera, and others. It took Mujica, already quite ill with hypertension, five months of 1983 to implement the idea of paintings becoming alive after closing hours to freely intermingle in the Prado. Two months after the book's publication the author, not yet seventy-four, succumbed. He must have had a premonition of his end, since death, the levity of the collection notwithstanding, is very much present in these tales.

It is seen in «La laguna» where frivolous Frenchmen embark on a strange vessel and are joined by the dramatized narrator, «el novelista»

---

[21] ALFRED J. MACADAM, *Modern Latin American Narratives* (Chicago, 1977), 150 pp.
[22] According to one of the obituaries, «El último encuentro», by MARÍA ESTHER VÁZQUEZ, *La Nación*, 29 April 1984.

(who again inserts himself in his creation), but are prevented from reaching the nether world by the morning opening of the museum. The story ends thus: «por esta vez (y por un pelo) el novelista se salvó de las fogatas y demás espantos infernales. Según especialistas, cuando allí se entra —no obstante el caso, tan literario, del Alighieri— es prácticamente imposible salir. Habrá que cuidarse.»[23]

The book is dedicated to the great museum, which must have been the writer's favorite and which was the setting for an episode in *Sergio*. Of course, the motif of pictures coming to life (and life becoming a tableau) has been a stand-by with Mujica Láinez. Yet in his last book the works of art are not chorus, as they were in *La casa*, nor narrator as in *El escarabajo;* they are a lyrical fantasy of the foreign novelist, who witnesses their awakening in a two-page overture rendered in italics. Then the stories, of very uneven length (from three to twenty-one pages) relate their secret nocturnal activities. These are most varied, both serious and mischievous, and completely disregard geographic and chronological disparities. Thus Mujica again used anachronism creatively. The assiduous tourist will identify many of the famous portraits and canvasses, animated by Mujica's creative wit, but it is not easy. The Museum is always «en obras», moving its collections. At a recent visit the suggestion that a guide be issued to accompany *Un novelista en el Museo del Prado* produced a benevolent smile from the vendors of such articles, who might even sell the guide as well as the book with the El Greco picture cover.

Mujica's animation of the work of art brings to life either the portrait itself or the individual that sat for it. This involves not only a duplication, because an image is left in the frame, but also an enactment or dramatization. This dramatic quality is often seen in the writer's technique. It is strongest when the fantasy is not limited to portraits. For example, the opening story, «Los dos carros», confronts the «Triunfo de Baco» of Cornelis de Vos with the «Carro de Heno» of Hieronimus Bosch in mass scenes of contrast. Less theological but no less ironic is the following tale, «El llanto y los remedios», in which the «Pharaoh's Daughter» of Veronese tries to console the «Gioconda» who is upset about the questionable authenticity of her Prado picture. In the end the charitable Egyptian princess goes on to Zurbarán's «Hercules» whose muscle cramps call for a devoted masseuse.

«Elegancia» is a beauty contest, which enables Mujica Láinez to pull out all his Modernist register of celebrities, finery, processions, etc., only to end up with the victory of the nudes, «Adam and Eve» by Dürer. In «Las dos hormigas» the two insects of «Disputa con los doctores en el templo» bother the human figures of the canvas. When one of them, or

---

[23] *Un novelista en el Museo del Prado* (Barcelona, 1984), pp. 128, henceforth to be cited in the text.

rather Veronese's Italian model, kills the ants, they are miraculously revived by the Christchild as the novelist sees behind the Boy and behind the artist God's «gratuita y simple bondad» (67).

In «La Bella Durmiente» the author again uses multiple levels of reality, as he had done in «El vampiro» of the *Crónicas*. It is a performance of a pantomime within a story which is being read in a painting. The organizer of the skit is the royal dwarf Acedo —the links to *Glosas, El laberinto,* and *El escarabajo* are obvious— who can insert himself into other pictures but has trouble finding suitable actors. The tale ends grotesquely when the «Danae», of Titian, is replaced by the «Monstrua», of Carreño de Miranda, who had a previous existence in Mujica's preceding novel.

In «La Corona» the Warrior of Van Dyck's painting sets out to find an angel missing from a Tiépolo picture. In the process the Warrior passes through Bosch's «Garden of Lust» where he observes «gimnasias del sexo», an «actividad harto trabajosa» (97f) and is himself seduced by a Hermaphrodite, all in typical Mujica Láinez manner. The Prado's pictorial society ladies also organize an entertainment for the children in «Zoológico», which suits the novelist's penchant for grotesque or chaotic enumeration. He returns to his favorite, El Greco, in «Amores», in which the Museum's Association of El Greco Caballeros questions the chastity of one of its officers who seems to have been seen with Goya's Maja. The president decides to investigate but the story's open ending merely reports the replacement of that presiding officer.

In addition to its overall Modernist concept, the book, as we should expect, is also full of Modernist details. For example, the Stygian waters of «La laguna» are described by the novelist in the typically Modernist phrase: «Su tornasolado azul le recuerda el de ciertas alas de mariposa» (126). The Modernist decorative-ironic use of religion might be seen in «La visita». It brings together the «Virgin of the Annunciation» of Giovanni da Fiésole with the somewhat neglected Virgins of the Early Spanish School downstairs. As a result, the multiple, variegated Madonnas set up a regular *tertulia* schedule. Goya's «Coloso» provides another surprising twist. He had terrified many other pictorial personages but the danger is removed when he is subjected to the brain surgery of a Bosch canvas and ends up a soprano.

In the final story, «El emperador», Carlos V leaves his Titian painting to meditate before Breughel's «Triunfo de la muerte» and then rides on in search of his own death. Thus the charming, somewhat funny book does in fact end on a serious note. Did Mujica Láinez foresee his own approaching death?

CONCLUSION

A SATIRICAL NEO-MODERNISM

When the Argentinian Mujica Láinez became one of the most widely read authors in Spain,[1] on account of a book with the broadest temporal and geographical coordinates; when he expressed his preference for living in the age of the Renaissance and the desire to spend extended periods in Paris or Venice (*Mundo,* 167), it was all consistent with everything he had achieved, written or said before — and the Modernists of the turn of the century would have endorsed his words. Borges, of course, concurred with Mujica Láinez, in the aforementioned Dialogue/Interview, and the two men thus acknowledged a cosmopolitanism, which one critic called «un europeísmo americano», characteristic of Argentine literature (Villena, 5). Theirs is an urban Argentina, which constantly looks to Europe, which turns its back on the Pampa and its vast ranches. «Yo no tengo una visión de la estancia», Mujica Láinez conceded,[2] and he confessed that he does not like the gauchesque *Martín Fierro (Mundo,* 60). It is an Argentina which considers herself different from Latin America, a continent starting somewhere near Córdoba and synthesized in *De milagros y de melancolías.* The latter is also the only book of Mujica Láinez with a mythical ambience, for he is, essentially, a writer of real, urban milieus.

His is a vision of a world just beyond its prime, a formula also applicable to the settings of his historical trilogy. As a somewhat déclassé scion of his country's once ruling oligarchy he could observe the remnants of a splendorous society both as an outsider and an insider. The result is a portrayal of the past which is both ironic and nostalgic. No wonder this portrayal found favor with a public in search of identity, and it still benefits from the current universal quest for roots. The commitment to the past, in addition to his aesthetic commitment, also distin-

---

[1] According to a survey of cultural life in Spain, in 1982, seen in the German «Lufthansa» Magazine, in January 1983.
[2] In the Sáenz Quesada interview, *Clarín,* 10 January 1980.

guishes Mujica Láinez from other contemporary writers who are clearly commited to the present.

However, Mujica Láinez, as we have seen, shared with many of today's writers, including Spanish American writers, a great concern with time. He lacked the philosophical depth of Sábato and the psychological profundity of Mallea; he once called the innovative Cortázar, who had spent most of his life in Europe, an excellent French writer who also writes good Spanish. Like Borges, Mujica Láinez —ten years younger than his octogenarian friend but equally independent— would not think of permanently leaving his beloved city for economic or political reasons, as did other men of leters.

Mujica Láinez's undeniable success with the reading public is not matched by a corresponding critical publicity, though. It is not that the writer's large corpus is reviewed unfavorably. Rather, it receives less attention than the works of more experimental or commited authors. This is attributable to a number of reasons, privately acknowledged by some critics: one is the writer's background —he may have satirized the past oligarchy more effectively than any of its social critics but he is felt to be part of it; another is a sort of envy— his novels and stories fared better than those of others who chose to ignore him; finally, the recurrent motif of homosexuality in his writings offended the real or pretended «machismo» of a sector of opinion.

Nevertheless, Mujica Láinez's success is no longer a mere Argentine phenomenon. His popularity in Spain, undoubtedly, owes as much to his style as to the universal themes of his works. In an interview, the writer conceded to the Spanish critic Villena that he had to create for himself an idiom without localisms, one with a vocabulary broader than that used by his countrymen but a language that at the same time would be comprehensible to all Spanish speakers.[3] Although not part of the «boom» of Latin American fiction, Mujica Láinez obviously benefitted from its aftermath in Spain, being, perhaps, the least exotic, most traditional, and most Spanish novelist from Hispanic America.

The closeness to Spain can be noted in his early and his most recent books. It is accompanied by a life-long affinity (apparently a family tradition) to British and Italian cultural values, not just to French ones as is the norm with Argentine intellectuals. These affinities may have contributed to Mujica Láinez's universal appeal, but his universality is seen even in one of his favorite topics, Buenos Aires, the world city, and in the constants of his works. Neither *El escarabajo* nor the books of his «Universalist Phase» are necessarily the most universal ones. Rather, I

---

[3] «Manuel Mujica Láinez entre la literatura y la vida», *Insula*, 34, Nos. 392-93 (1979), 1 and 22.

would term *La casa* his book of potentially widest acclaim[4] and its translation into English is long overdue.

The writer's universal constants, as shown in the present study, are almost repetitive. His protagonists are losers. The men usually struggle in vain and the women, who may be domineering, frivolous, or just unfortunate, are often destroyed. Love and achievement is followed by loss and defeat. Man and his passions are always the same in all places and epochs. This pessimistic view of a world with little room for goodness would be intolerable, were it not for beauty and art which make life not only liveable but also meaningful.

The pervasive aestheticism in Mujica Láinez's production approximates him to the Spanish American Modernists of the turn of the century. This has not remained unnoticed[5] but hardly been demonstrated in any detail. The author himself does not appear eager to discuss it; perhaps it seems too academic to him. He is definitely not an experimenter; even his use of uncommon narrators is not particularly innovative, especially when they sound very much like the author. But consciously or not, Mujica Láinez followed patterns of an earlier period, as seen almost to excess in these pages.

His narrative stress is on situations rather than on action or character. The latter tend to be representatives of epochs. They are either artists or involved with the arts — which enables the writer to dwell on splendor. Objects rather than man have transcendence. Narrative progress is by a series of scenes or vignettes. Finally, the passion for the pictorial is accompanied by a passion for language, manifested in long, indirect, polished periods or in lyrical prose. Cruz, who may be the only critic to discern a difference, affirms that Mujica Láinez has transformed the Modernist prose of earlier days. «La ha aligerado, la ha argentinizado» (*Mundo*, 195).

In spite of all thematic, structural, and stylistic similarities, there is an obvious dissimilarity between the texts of previous generations and the works of Mujica Láinez: satire, which is already seen in some of the writings of Rubén Darío, José Asunción Silva, and others is used consistently and heavily by the contemporary Argentinian. Therefore Mujica Láinez should be called a «Satirical Neo-Modernist». This label, of course, does not conflict with that of a «classic», used in an obituary by Juan Carlos Ghiano, of the Argentine Academy. Ghiano termed Mujica a writer

---

[4] The author himself calls it «uno de mis libros más logrados por lo que tiene de imaginativo y de poético» (*Mundo*, 75).
[5] ALBA OMIL DE PIEROLA, «Mujica Láinez y las posibilidades de la novela», *La novela iberoamericana* (Caracas, 1968), 298. Memoria del XIII Congreso de Literatura Iberoamericana. Also CRUZ (*Mundo*, 191) and others.

«para ser estudiado en clase, pero también situado sobre los sorpresivos vaivenes de las modas literarias».[6]

Indeed, I can foresee a time when only specialists will be concerned with the extreme innovators of today, while the readers of many lands will still enjoy some of Mujica Láinez's best fictions. Those most likely to be remembered are *La casa,* of the Saga of Buenos Aires; *El laberinto,* of the universalist trilogy; *Crónicas reales,* of the linked novellas; plus some of the stories that are already appearing in anthologies.

---

[6] *La Nación,* 29 April 1984.

BIBLIOGRAPHY

PRIMARY SOURCES*

1. NOVELS AND LINKED NOVELLAS:

Bomarzo. Buenos Aires: Editorial Sudamericana, 1962.
La casa. Buenos Aires: Editorial Sudamericana, 1954.
Cecil. Buenos Aires: Editorial Sudamericana, 1972.
Los cisnes. Buenos Aires: Editorial Sudamericana, 1977.
Crónicas reales. Buenos Aires: Editorial Sudamericana, 1967.
De milagros y de melancolías. Buenos Aires: Editorial Sudamericana, 1968.
Don Galaz de Buenos Aires. Buenos Aires: Imp. Francisco Colombo, 1938.
El escarabajo. Barcelona: Plaza y Janés, 1982.
El gran teatro. Buenos Aires: Editorial Sudamericana, 1953.
Los ídolos. Buenos Aires: Editorial Sudamericana, 1953.
Invitados en El Paraíso. Buenos Aires: Editorial Sudamericana, 1957.
El laberinto. Buenos Aires: Editorial Sudamericana, 1974.
Sergio. Buenos Aires: Editorial Sudamericana, 1976.
El unicornio. Buenos Aires: Editorial Sudamericana, 1965.
El viaje de los siete demonios. Buenos Aires: Editorial Sudamericana, 1974.
Los viajeros. Buenos Aires: Editorial Sudamericana, 1955.

2. SHORT STORIES

Aquí vivieron. Buenos Aires: Editorial Sudamericana, 1949.
El brazalete y otros cuentos. Buenos Aires: Editorial Sudamericana, 1978.
Misteriosa Buenos Aires. Buenos Aires: Editorial Sudamericana, 1950.
Un novelista en el Museo del Prado. Barcelona: Seix Barral, 1984.

3. LIBRETTO AND POETRY

Bomarzo, Opera (bilingual). New York: Boosey and Hawkes, 1967.
Canto a Buenos Aires. Buenos Aires: Guillermo Kraft, 1943.
Cincuenta sonetos de Shakespeare. Buenos Aires: Ediciones Culturales Argentinas, 1963.

---

* Not including editions of other writers, translations of plays, art books, and «urban travel books».

4. ESSAYS, ARTICLES, AND INTERVIEWS

Glosas castellanas. Buenos Aires: Librería y Editorial «La Facultad», 1936.
El mundo de Manuel Mujica Láinez: Conversaciones con María Esther Vázquez. Buenos Aires: Editorial de Belgrano, 1983.
Placeres y fatigas de los viajes. Crónicas de viaje aparecidas en *La Nación*, 1935-1977. Buenos Aires: Editorial Sudamericana, 1983 (I), 1984 (II).
Los porteños. Buenos Aires: Ediciones Librería «La Ciudad», 1979.

5. BIOGRAPHIES

Miguel Cané (Padre). Buenos Aires: C.E.P.A., 1942.
Vida de Anastasio el Pollo. Buenos Aires: Emecé, 1948.
Vida de Aniceto el Gallo. Buenos Aires: Emecé, 1943.

6. ANTHOLOGIES AND COLLECTIONS

Antología general e introducción a la obra de Manuel Mujica Láinez. Madrid: Ediciones Felmar, 1976.
Cuentos de Buenos Aires. Buenos Aires: Huemul, 1972.
Manuel Mujica Láinez. Buenos Aires: Ediciones Culturales Argentina, 1962.
Obras completas I. Buenos Aires: Editorial Sudamericana, 1978.
Obras completas II. Buenos Aires: Editorial Sudamericana, 1979.
Obras completas III. Buenos Aires: Editorial Sudamericana, 1980.
Obras completas IV. Buenos Aires: Editorial Sudamericana, 1981.
Obras completas V. Buenos Aires: Editorial Sudamericana, 1983.
Páginas de Manuel Mujica Láinez seleccionadas por el autor. Buenos Aires: Editorial Celtia, 1982.
El poeta perdido y otros relatos. Buenos Aires: Centro Editor de América Latina, 1981.

7. TRANSLATIONS (ENGLISH)

Bomarzo. Tr. by Gregory Rabassa. New York: Simon and Schuster, 1969.
The Wandering Unicorn. Tr. by Mary Fitton. Toronto: Lester and Orpen Dennys, 1982. Also, London, 1983; New York, 1983.

MAJOR SECONDARY SOURCES

1. BOOKS

CRUZ, JORGE: *Genio y figura de Manuel Mujica Láinez.* Buenos Aires: Eudeba, 1978.
   No. 31 in the University of Buenos Aires «Genio y figura» Series. Conforms to the pattern of providing bio-bibliographical information, with illustrations and a few anthological selections. Somewhat anecdotal but the most complete coverage to date of publication.
FONT, EDUARDO: *Realidad y fantasía en la narrativa de Manuel Mujica Láinez (1949-1962).* Madrid: José Porrúa Turanzas, 1976.
   An updated UCLA dissertation; provides, within the limits implied in its title, a good critical survey, with emphasis on the writer's first story collections and three of his novels.

2. INTRODUCTIONS, ARTICLES, AND INTERVIEWS

CARSUZÁN, MARÍA EMMA: In *Manuel Mujica Láinez,* one of the official sesquicentennial publications of 1962. A fifty-page overview of the first half of the writer's production, barely reaching *Bomarzo,* followed by a hundred-page anthology and useful bio-bibliographical data; illustrated.

CASTELLANOS, CARMELINA: *Tres nombres en la novela argentina.* Santa Fe: Colmegna, 1967.
Mujica Láinez section devoted mainly to the Saga of Buenos Aires.

GHIANO, JUAN CARLOS: In *Cuentos de Buenos Aires.* Introduction to the anthology based on the writer's first two story collections, but not strictly confined to them. A fifty-seven page critical study and, prior to Villena's, the best.

MARANI, ALMA NOVELLA: «El renacimiento en Manuel Mujica Láinez», *Studi di letteratura ispano-americana,* 11 (1981). Università degli Studi di Venezia. (Milano: Cisalpino-Goliárdica.)
A substantial exploration of the links between the contemporary Argentinian and Ariosto and Cellini.

MATAMORO, BLAS: «El crepúsculo de los señores», in *Literatura y oligarquía.* Buenos Aires: Libros del Tercer Mundo, 1975.
A balanced view of Mujica Láinez as the chronicler of a vanishing class, written by a man of the left.

OMIL DE PIEROLA, ALBA: «Mujica Láinez y las posibilidades de la novela», *La novela iberoamericana.* Caracas: Universidad Central, 1968. XIII Congreso Internacional de Literatura Iberoamericana.
Perhaps the first allusion to the novelist's Modernist tendencies.

SCHANZER, GEORGE O.: «De la gloria de don Ramiro al desengaño de don Ginés», *Romance Literary Studies,* Homage to Harvey L. Johnson. Potomac, MD: José Porrúa Turanzas, 1979.
On the evolution of Mujica Láinez's satirical treatment of history.

VÁZQUEZ, MARÍA ESTHER: *El mundo de Manuel Mujica Láinez.* Buenos Aires: Editorial de Belgrano, 1983.
Conversaciones with the writer on his inspirations, his works, his preferences, and his technique. Very informal.

VILLENA, LUIS ANTONIO DE: In *Antología general e introducción a la obra de Manuel Mujica Láinez.* Madrid: Felmar, 1976.
A twenty-two page critical evaluation, which precedes a three hundred page sampling of novels, novellas, and stories. The most sensitive and best study to date.

VILLORDO, OSCAR HERMES: Introduction to *Páginas de Manuel Mujica Láinez seleccionadas por el autor.* Buenos Aires: Editorial Celtia, 1982.
An updated overview, on the order of Cruz's, for a broader audience.

INDEX

Acedo, Diego de, 141.
Adler, Alfred, 82, 126.
Aldazábal, Pablo, 97.
Alvear, Marcelo T., 16.
Alvear Ortiz Basualdo, Ana María de, 16, 23, 140.
Araoz, Eugenio, 63, 68.
Aretino, Pietro, 82.
Arévalo Martínez, Rafael, 125.
Ariosto, Ludovico, 83, 133, 149.
Aristophanes, 138.
Ascasubi, Hilario, 18, 40, 41, 42, 43, 44, 45.
Azorín (José Martínez Ruiz), 17, 22, 29, 102, 137.

Barbieri, Vicente, 63.
Basaldúa, Héctor, 21, 37, 38, 46.
Bashkirtsev, Marie, 16.
Bedoian, Juan, 132.
Bernhardt, Sarah, 28, 138.
Blanes, Juan Manuel, 39.
Bogliano, Jorge, 35.
Bonet, Carmelo, 33.
Borges, Jorge Luis, 11, 15, 16, 19, 20, 21, 23, 25, 37, 39, 42, 63, 67, 85, 86, 96, 105, 129, 132, 143, 144.
Bosch, Hieronymus, 105, 141, 142.
Breughel, Pieter, 105, 142.
Bullrich, Silvina, 102.
Bulwer-Lytton, Edward, 105.
Buonarroti, Michelangelo, 138.
Burgess, Anthony, 133.

Caesar, Julius, 138.
Calderón de la Barca, Pedro, 124, 127.
Cambaceres, Eugenio, 73.
Campo, Estanislao del, 18, 40, 43, 44, 45, 57, 127.
Campos, Jorge, 85, 127.
Cané, Miguel, Jr., 18, 36.
Cané, Miguel, Sr., 18, 36, 37, 129.
Capestany, Cecilia Delacre, 12.
Carreño de Miranda, Juan, 142.
Carlos V, 31, 83, 142.

Carpentier, Alejo, 96.
Carsuzán, María Emma, 73, 78, 149.
Castellanos, Carmelina de, 80, 149.
Cellini, Benvenuto, 75, 82, 83, 149.
Cervantes Saavedra, Miguel de, 28, 29, 30, 31, 83, 97, 99, 110.
Chrétien de Troyes, 126.
Claudel, Paul, 120.
Columbus, Christopher, 111.
Cortázar, Julio, 11, 21, 92, 144.
Cruz, Jorge, 24, 25, 26, 27, 35, 41, 42, 45, 46, 83, 89, 91, 103, 110, 113, 132, 144, 145, 148, 149.

Dalí, Salvador, 105.
Dante Alighieri, 105, 141.
Darío, Rubén, 24, 51, 56, 92, 96, 106, 112, 119, 145.
Dürer, Albrecht, 141.

Eliot, T. S., 63.
Eschenbach, Wolfram von, 126.
Estrada, Santiago, 18.
Euripides, 118, 120.

Farnese, Julia, 83.
Felipe V, 49.
Figari, Pedro, 20, 38, 46.
Fini, Leonor, 114.
Fitton, Mary, 86, 132, 148.
Flaubert, Gustave, 79.
Font, Eduardo, 12, 48, 63, 68, 78, 80, 82, 89, 103, 148.
Foster, David William, 85, 103, 107.
Foster, Virginia Ramos, 96.
Freud, Sigmund, 82, 126, 135.
Frondizi, Arturo, 21.

Gambartes, Leonidas, 21, 46.
Garibaldi, Giuseppe, 41.
Garassa, Delfín Leocadio, 113.
Garay, Juan de, 15, 38, 48, 128.
García Lorca, Federico, 26.

García Márquez, Gabriel, 92, 98, 124.
Garcilaso de la Vega, 83, 102.
Gerchunoff, Alberto, 26, 132.
Ghiano, Juan Carlos, 47, 53, 63, 73, 80, 92, 97, 145, 149.
Gigli, Adelaida, 61.
Ginastera, Alberto, 21, 79, 123.
Giovanni da Fiésole, 142.
Gittes, Katherine Slater, 139.
Goldoni, Carlos, 105.
Gómez de Quevedo, Francisco, 106.
Gonzaga, Julia, 83.
González Lanuza, Eduardo, 63, 68, 123, 124, 127.
Gounod, Charles François, 70.
Goya, Francisco José de, 142.
Greco, El (Domenicos Theotocopoulos), 27, 30, 52, 71, 100, 101, 134, 136, 137, 141, 142.
Greenland, Colin, 133.
Groussac, Paul, 18.

Hanke, Lewis, 15, 16, 17.
Heine, Heinrich, 123, 126.
Heker, Liliana, 139.
Heliogabalus, 111, 112.
Henneberg, Josephine von, 80, 81.
Hernández, José, 45, 143.
Hidalgo, Bartolomé, 41, 44.
Hugo, Victor, 71, 133.
Huidobro, Vicente, 139.

Irigoyen, Hipólito, 16, 26.

Jaimes Freyre, Mireya, 78.
Juana la Loca, 111.
Jung, Carl Gustav, 82.

Krieble, Gladys, 63.

Lagos, Alberto, 21.
Láinez Varela, Lucía, 15, 24.
Lanusse, Alejandro, 22.
Larreta, Enrique Rodríguez, 18, 26, 27, 32, 33, 34, 35, 43, 62, 100, 102, 128, 132.
Lerner, Isaías, 89.
Lewald, H. Ernest, 15.
López, Lucio Vicente, 44.
Lotto, Lorenzo, 83.
Lugones, Leopoldo, 25.
Louis XVI, 24, 54.

MacAdam, Aldrich, 115.
MacAdam, Alfred J., 139, 140.

McGann, Thomas, 15, 17.
Mailer, Norman, 138.
Mallarmé, Stephane, 119.
Mallea, Eduardo, 19, 26, 144.
Manrique, Jorge, 60, 96.
Mao Tse-tung, 106.
Marani, Alma Novella, 83, 149.
Marivaux, Pierre Carlet de, 90.
Martí, José, 55.
Martín de Porres, 102.
Martínez Estrada, Ezequiel, 17.
Matamoro, Blas, 26, 139, 140, 149.
Mena, Juan de, 99.
Mikulski, Richard, 73.
Milton, John, 105.
Miranda, Luis de, 56.
Mistral, Gabriela (Lucila Godoy Alcayaga), 42.
Mitre, Adolfo, 22, 98.
Molière (Jean Baptiste Poquelin), 16, 21, 85.
Mujica Farías, Manuel, 15, 24.
Musset, Alfred de, 42, 120.

Napoleon (I) Bonaparte, 72.
Napoleon III, 72.
Nefertari, 137.
Neruda, Pablo, 96.
Nervo, Amado, 52.
Noel, Martín Alberto, 139.

Ocampo, Victoria, 128.
Omil de Pierola, Alba, 107, 145, 149.
Onganía, Juan Carlos, 21.
Orgambide, Pedro, 52.
Orsini, Pier Francesco, 80, 81.
Ortega y Gasset, José, 105, 115.

Palma, Ricardo, 56.
Paul III, 75.
Perón, Juan Domingo, 17, 18, 20, 21, 22, 23, 67, 129.
Philip II, 33.
Polo, Marco, 26, 138.
Potence, Jaime, 70.
Proust, Marcel, 43, 63, 127.
Puyrredón, Prilidiano, 50.

Quiroga, Facundo, 41.

Rabassa, Gregory, 80, 148.
Rabelais, François, 86, 96, 97.
Racine, Jean Baptiste, 16, 70, 71, 98.
Rais, Gilles de, 104.
Ramses II, 137.

INDEX

Revol, Enrique, 93.
Rilke, Rainer Maria, 71, 91.
Rimbaud, Arthur, 71.
Roggiano, Alfredo, 59.
Rojas, Santiago, 16.
Rojas Guardia, Pablo, 85.
Romero, Francisco, 129.
Rosales, Carlos, 49.
Rosas, Juan Manuel de, 36, 39, 41, 44, 50, 54, 56, 129.

Sábato, Ernesto, 19, 144.
Sáenz Peña, Roque, 15.
Sáenz Quesada, María, 53, 88, 122, 143.
Saladin, 87.
Salas, Horacio, 112.
San Martín, Juan José de, 54.
Schanzer, George O., 32, 81, 86, 92, 98, 100, 103, 139, 149.
Schwartz, Kessel, 112.
Scobie, James, 15, 16.
Sessa, Aldo, 127.
Shakespeare, William, 20, 21, 59, 85, 90, 91, 126, 131, 147.
Silva, José Asunción, 145.
Soldi, Raúl, 21.
Stevenson, Robert Louis, 105, 133.
Storni, Alfonsina, 28.
Sully Prudhomme, René, 119.
Swift, Jonathan, 93, 97.

Tejeda, Luis de, 102.
Teresa of Avila, 102.
Tiépolo, Giovanni Battista, 142.
Titian (Tiziano Vecellio), 142.

Valera, Juan, 103.
Valle Inclán, Ramón de, 23.

Van Dyck, Anthony, 25, 142.
Varela, Florencio, 37, 41, 129.
Varela, Juan Cruz, 37, 39.
Varela, Juan Cruz II, 129.
Varela, Justa, 83.
Vázquez, María Esther, 80, 106, 133, 140, 148, 149.
Vega, Lope de, 100, 101, 102.
Velázquez, Diego Rodríguez de Silva, 117, 138.
Vélez de Guevara, Luis, 127.
Verlaine, Paul, 126.
Veronese, Paolo, 141, 142.
Victorica, Miguel Carlos, 21, 46, 74.
Villena, Luis Antonio de, 11, 57, 63, 68, 85, 89, 90, 93, 97, 106, 109, 112, 124, 143, 144, 149.
Villordo, Oscar Hermes, 21, 89, 117, 121, 132, 149.
Viñas, David, 67, 68, 69.
Voltaire (François Marie Arouet), 56, 135.
Vos, Cornelis de, 141.

Wagman, Anita, 12, 84, 89, 96, 103.
Wagner, Richard, 91, 122, 123, 124, 125, 126, 127.
Whitelow, Guillermo, 136.
Wilde, Eduardo, 18.
Wordsworth, William, 58.
Wrede, Maria Elizabeth, 42.

Yahni, Roberto, 52.
Yeats, William Butler, 118, 119.

Zúñiga, Francesillo de, 31.
Zurbarán, Francisco, 141.